WE ARE GEELONG

THE PICTORIAL STORY OF GEELONG'S CAMPAIGN TO WIN A 10TH VFL/AFL PREMIERSHIP

INTRODUCTION BY CRAIG DRUMMOND, PRESIDENT, GEELONG FOOTBALL CLUB
WORDS BY PETER DI SISTO, DAN EDDY, ANDREW GIGACZ, GEOFF SLATTERY
PHOTOS BY AFL PHOTOS

Hardie Grant
BOOKS

WINNERS: The premier team, with coach Chris Scott, celebrates after the Premiership Cup was presented.

COVER PHOTO BY MICHAEL WILSON, AFL PHOTOS

CONTENTS

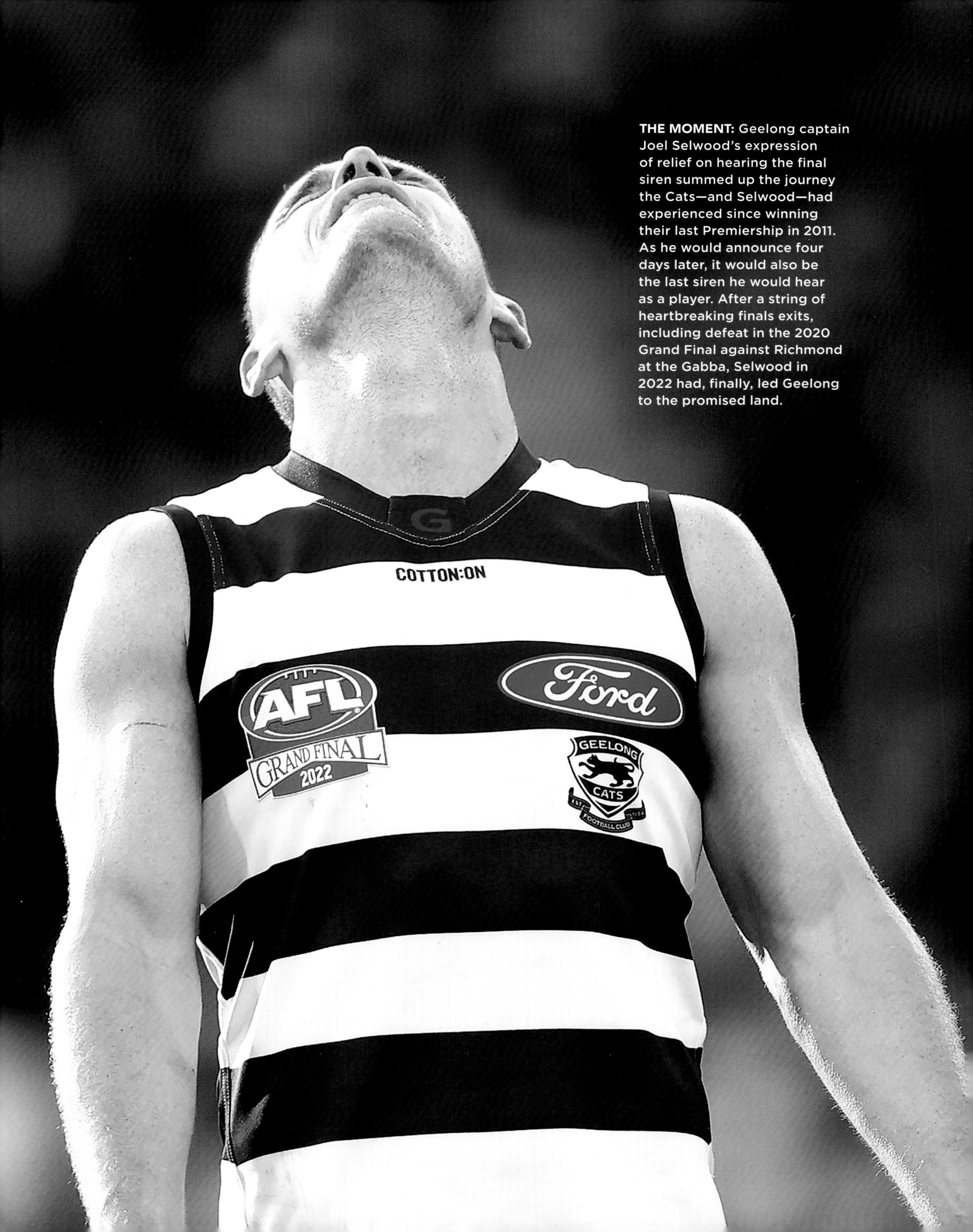

THE MOMENT: Geelong captain Joel Selwood's expression of relief on hearing the final siren summed up the journey the Cats—and Selwood—had experienced since winning their last Premiership in 2011. As he would announce four days later, it would also be the last siren he would hear as a player. After a string of heartbreaking finals exits, including defeat in the 2020 Grand Final against Richmond at the Gabba, Selwood in 2022 had, finally, led Geelong to the promised land.

HEROES IN HOOPS: Geelong's 2022 team was as dominant as any Premiership side in recent seasons—its teamwork and culture the envy of the competition. The Cats won 18 of 22 home and away matches, earned the McClelland Trophy as minor premiers, and saw five players (Tom Stewart, Jeremy Cameron, Tom Hawkins, Tyson Stengle and Mark Blicavs) selected in the All-Australian team. Cameron polled 19 Brownlow Medal votes—the most of any key forward—to finish in the top 10, and shared the 'Carji' Greeves Medal with Cam Guthrie, Isaac Smith won the Norm Smith Medal, Chris Scott took a second Jock McHale Medal as Premiership coach, and Joel Selwood set new VFL/AFL benchmarks for games played as captain and finals played. Quite simply, this team did it all.

BACK ROW (FROM LEFT): Luke Dahlhaus, Quinton Narkle, Sam Simpson, Jed Bews, Gary Rohan, Sam Menegola, Isaac Smith, Shaun Higgins, Brad Close, Brandan Parfitt.
THIRD ROW: Mitch Knevitt, Jake Kolodjashnij, Esava Ratugolea, Paul Tsapatolis, Shannon Neale, Jonathon Ceglar, Toby Conway, Sam De Koning, Rhys Stanley, Jeremy Cameron, Jack Henry.
SECOND ROW: Gryan Miers, Zach Tuohy, Tom Hawkins, Tom Stewart, Joel Selwood, (captain), Chris Scott, (coach), Patrick Dangerfield, Mitch Duncan, Mark Blicavs, Mark O'Connor, Cam Guthrie.
FRONT ROW: Tom Atkins, Cooper Whyte, James Willis, Flynn Kroeger, Max Holmes, Nick Stevens, Cooper Stephens, Zach Guthrie, Oliver Dempsey, Francis Evans, Tyson Stengle.

AFL
Ford
GEELONG
CATS
FOOTBALL CLUB
AFL PREMIERS 2022
COTTON:ON

FROM THE SUMMIT: After finally winning the Premiership he'd waited some 303 games and 15 seasons with both Adelaide (2008-15) and Geelong to accomplish, Patrick Dangerfield said post-match that he'd reached football's Everest. The way he celebrated with the Premiership Cup, surrounded by delirious Geelong fans, it was clear he enjoyed the view from the summit.

17:54
20 · 13 · 133
8 · 4 · 52
COTTON:ON
AFL
GRAND FINAL
2022
Ford
GEELONG
CATS
TOYOTA
TOYOTA

KINSHIP: Given their careers at Geelong ran parallel for 16 seasons (305 games together for 217 wins), it was no surprise to see best mates Tom Hawkins and Joel Selwood share a moment with the 2022 Premiership Cup after both had paved the way to glory with fine displays in the Grand Final. Hawkins's daughters Arabella and Primrose look perplexed at their father's outburst of emotion, but they'll have plenty of stories to tell from such a magical day.

TOYOTA FOOTY. OH WHAT A FEELING
AFL PREMIERS 2022

ENTERTAINER: A headline act throughout his nine-season, 171-game career with the GWS GIANTS, Jeremy Cameron arrived at Geelong with plenty of expectations placed on his shoulders. After 39 games and 104 goals in the blue and white hoops—2.67 goals per game—Cameron has well and truly justified his hefty price tag. Two goals on Grand Final day proved the precursor to an evening no one at Geelong will ever forget. Reflecting on his journey, Cameron said: "I have only been here for two years—what they have been able to do for a long time before that is incredible, isn't it? It's funny. You sort of sit back and go: if I go to Geelong ... I knew they were old, but I knew they had the players who just want to win, players who just want to step up." Later in the week, Cameron's stellar season was confirmed, when he shared the 'Carji' Greeves Medal—the club's best and fairest award—with Cameron Guthrie, each polling 113 votes.

TOO GOOD: After Geelong's heavy loss in the 2021 Preliminary Final—it was later revealed there were many players who had entered the game unwell—it seemed the club's long run of success might be over. The Cats were, it was said, too old to regenerate. That thinking carried through to the Grand Final, with the oldest team to take the field for any VFL/AFL match, not just a final, the critics were suggesting Geelong would be too old and too slow for the more youthful Sydney Swans. But, as Chris Scott's men have proven time and time again, age does not weary them. The Cats outran, out-bustled, out-thought and totally outplayed the Swans on the way to a mammoth 81-point victory. The fan carrying the banner got it just right: Too old? Too slow? No—just too damn good.

GEELONG
SELWOOD
14
CATS
2 OLD
2 SLOW
2 GOOD
PREMIERS
ISC
PREMIERS

THANKS PRES: Geelong president Craig Drummond shares the exhilaration that follows a Premiership victory with Patrick Dangerfield. Drummond, who has been on the Geelong board since 2011, took over the presidency from Colin Carter in January 2021 and has overseen significant change in his short time in charge, including the smooth transition of chief executive from the exemplary Brian Cook to former Geelong player and football manager (and AFL football manager) Steve Hocking. Drummond had retired as chief executive of Medibank in mid-2021, after a long career in the finance sector. After the victory, the lifelong Cats fan told *The Age:* "We try to appoint great people. They get on with their job and we get on with ours to make sure we keep away all that off-field noise you hear at other organisations." That truly has been the mark of a run of Geelong's presidents—from Ron Hovey, Frank Costa, Carter and now Drummond—to concentrate on the business of making—and keeping—Geelong great.

THE ULTIMATE REWARD

There were 4012 days between our 2011 Premiership and our most recent triumph at the MCG on September 24, 2022.

Was either victory more satisfying than the other? That's difficult to say, as both were extraordinary in their own way, but what I'm most proud of is what happened in between those dates.

How our club evolved, how it challenged itself, how everyone from Steve Hocking, Chris Scott, Joel Selwood and all of our staff—right throughout the club—never stopped working and they never stopped dreaming.

The victory on September 24 was the ultimate reward for our club's patience, perseverance and bravery—for the Geelong way, our Kardinia spirit.

We had our knockers. Indeed, the too old and too slow refrain isn't new. But we stayed connected in the calm and chaos and each year we reassessed our way forward, as all good organisations do.

Ultimately, the 2022 celebrations were sweeter for the kind of club we have become in the years between the Premierships.

Consider: we have won four flags in 16 years and our coach has a 73 per cent-winning record. Add to that 15 finals series' in the past 16 years, and a top-four finish in 13 of those years.

This isn't to brag or boast, but it's a tribute to our club and the people in it, to our guiding principles and the club's appetite for considered risk, and the emotional toll that putting ourselves forward to challenge every year takes.

Our guiding principles have shaped and fortified our down-to-earth approach. We've worked really hard to make our club a place people want to be a part of, and because of that we've attracted really good people, and it's because of our people I'm writing this introduction to *We Are Geelong*.

I'm proud; not just because we won the Premiership, but how we won.

I'm proud of the way Jeremy Cameron celebrated his teammates' goals as hard as he did his own. I'm proud of the way our staff at the MCG rode every bump with our players on the ground. I'm proud of the reactions in the coaches' box to the Brandan Parfitt and Sam De Koning goals and I'm proud of all the hard work and sacrifices the playing group and their families have made over several years.

It's often said a champion team will always beat a team of champions and this may be so, but you can be both. Oh, we have some champions in our team, but collectively they played each and every week like a champion team and we should all be very, very proud of that.

It's often said that when the Cats win, the whole town wins.

Indeed we are as intimately connected as any team can be with its hometown. But the club doesn't win without our members and supporters, and my heart was full as I saw the celebrations wind through every Geelong street, every venue, and every backyard up and down the coast.

I even heard a story of a proposal at three-quarter time of the Grand Final. Congratulations to Jeff and Jane if you're reading this; football, it must be said, can do extraordinary things for people.

In an increasingly disconnected, digital world, football remains the constant that brings us all together. If you were at Kardinia Park on the Sunday after the Grand Final cheering our triumphant heroes, you were among our winning team.

But as sweet as they are, and they are very, very sweet, a Premiership isn't the only measure of success.

I'm proud that we gave everyone a chance to feel that shot of hope, that rush of adrenaline as they threw on their scarf each weekend and walked toward the bright lights of GMHBA Stadium or the MCG, hearts full of hope and heads full of dreams.

I'm proud that we continue to give all of our players, members and supporters the chance, each and every year, to feel like we do today. **G**

Craig Drummond
President, Geelong Football Club
October, 2022

KEEPING THE FAITH

As he reflected on another season lost, Geelong coach Chris Scott knew that change was required at the end of 2021. Since winning a premiership in his first season, 2011, Scott had led the Cats into the finals in all but one of the next 10 seasons (2015), but on each occasion they had fallen short of the ultimate prize. Two Elimination Final defeats, a semi-final loss, five Preliminary Final exits and a shattering loss to Richmond in the 2020 Grand Final (after leading by 15 points at half-time) had critics suggesting that Scott, despite holding the best home and away winning record of any coach (with more than 80 games) in League history, couldn't get it done when the heat was at its fiercest during finals time.

Even the supremely positive Scott questioned whether he'd taken his men to the well so many times, for so little silverware, that perhaps the time was nigh to hand the reins over to a new leader with a fresh approach. He put it to his senior players, seeking guidance on what was best for the group and the club, going forward. "I made it hard for them," Scott revealed after the 2022 Grand Final. "I said if you have any doubt at all you have to tell me. It was a bigger group than just Joel (Selwood) and Pat (Dangerfield) and I have done a version of that every year, but at the end of '21—in particular—they were emphatic, and the support was the basis of my drive in 2022." But, he conceded, if the players "had hesitated" he would have considered walking. "[It was about] whether we could do it and if we couldn't, we needed to change tack; and maybe part of that change involved me."

In the 2021 Preliminary Final, the Cats looked old and slow, with a stale game plan and some senior warriors seemingly on their last legs, against a Melbourne team riding a wave of momentum on the way to a drought-breaking premiership. Acknowledging new ideas were required, there was a turnover of support staff at Kardinia Park with the departures of line coaches Corey Enright, Matthew Knights and Matthew Scarlett. In came the recently retired Eddie Betts, plus former Cats Matthew Egan, James Kelly and Josh Jenkins. The new brains trust devised a more attacking, risk-taking style to, in Scott's words, "put more pressure on the opposition".

Not only did this new approach increase Geelong's scoring output (from 81 points per game in 2021 to 99 per game in 2022), but their stingy defence was even more impassable. After letting in just 69 points per game in 2021, that figure dipped to 66 in 2022.

During the end-of-season trade period, recruiter Stephen Wells pulled a surprise by signing delisted free agent Tyson Stengle, whose off-field troubles at Adelaide had seemingly ended his AFL career in 2020. They also traded for Hawthorn ruckman Jonathon Ceglar as a back-up for Rhys Stanley but lost up-and-coming winger Jordan Clark to Fremantle. Stengle, in particular, would alter Scott's forward structure, providing even greater fire power and unpredictability. With high-priced recruit Jeremy Cameron getting on top of injury woes, which had greatly impacted his first season at Geelong, there was suddenly a whole new look about the Cats' forward half, which also contained sharpshooter Gary Rohan and the opportunists Gryan Miers and Brad Close.

In defence, 21-year-old Sam De Koning, who had played a solitary game in 2021, emerged as one of the finds of the season. His intercept marking complemented the work of one of the League's best exponents of the craft, Tom Stewart. De Koning would ultimately finish runner-up to Collingwood's Nick Daicos in the NAB AFL Rising Star Award. Others to have breakout seasons were Zach Guthrie, who finally stepped out of his older brother Cam's shadow, tight-checking defender Jack Henry, hardball winner Tom Atkins, running machine Max Holmes, and Indigenous utility Brandan Parfitt.

When the Cats belted Essendon in the opening round—itself a team with lofty, but ultimately unfounded expectations heading into the 2022 season—a summer of question and doubt (particularly externally) was quickly shelved. And despite a bumpy start to the year which saw Geelong sitting seventh after nine rounds, everything began to click as they ticked off win after win. Remarkably, a team that appeared too old, too slow, too stale under Scott just months earlier, had charged to the top of the AFL ladder and, entering the finals, had won 13 successive games. **G**

Dan Eddy

STATEMENT: Opening the season against Essendon at the MCG in round one, the Cats sent out an early warning to the competition, leading throughout to win by 66 points. Patrick Dangerfield (pictured after the game) set the tone from the outset with 22 disposals and nine inside-50s in the first half alone, earning himself the Tom Wills Award for best on ground. Other dominant ball-gatherers included Brandan Parfitt (32 disposals and 11 clearances) and skipper Joel Selwood (27 disposals and six clearances). Although it was the Bombers who were forced to lick their wounds, it wasn't all smooth sailing for Geelong either, with star forward Jeremy Cameron subbed out early after a heavy bump in the first quarter. Cameron was sent to hospital for scans on his ribs but would be declared fit to play the following week.

NEW RECRUIT: After a controversial end to his time with the Adelaide Crows (14 games from 2018-20 and various charges including drink driving), which followed a stint with Richmond (two games from 2017-18), talented small forward Tyson Stengle, (pictured here with Tom Stewart) spent the 2021 season re-establishing his passion and commitment to football at his original SANFL club, Woodville-West Torrens. The Eagles won the 2021 SANFL premiership over Glenelg to secure back-to-back flags for the first time in the club's history (with Stengle booting three goals) by which time Geelong's recruiting guru Stephen Wells had come calling. Stengle soon signed with the Cats as a delisted free agent and, with guidance from former Adelaide teammate Eddie Betts, now in a mentoring/development coaching role at Geelong, kickstarted his remarkable rebirth in the team's first-round thrashing of Essendon. Stengle, along with Tom Hawkins, kicked four goals in a stunning debut, a precursor to what would become a comeback season like no other.

'BUDDY' BLOW: The round two clash with the Sydney Swans, on a Friday night at the SCG, will forever be remembered for Lance 'Buddy' Franklin's 1000th goal and the dramatic on-field scenes that erupted the moment the milestone kick left Buddy's boot and sailed through the big sticks. For the neutral supporter, the result seemed secondary but for Geelong, the 30-point defeat was a disappointing performance against the young and rising Swans. Coach Chris Scott said after the game: "It was a bit of a strange night from our perspective. It almost looked like a wet-weather game for us. The problem was it didn't look like a wet-weather game for them. But it's not often you play poorly, get beaten by 30-odd points and [still manage to] have more scoring shots and inside-50s. So, it was a bit strange." One Cat who did handle the conditions well was Brad Close (here celebrating with Jeremy Cameron), who with four goals and 18 disposals was the only multiple goalkicker for his side.

COTTON ON
AFL
Ford

COTTON:ON
Ford
AFL
AFL
COTTON:ON

'JEZZA': With six goals under lights at the MCG, Jeremy 'Jezza' Cameron was the matchwinner in Geelong's stunning come from behind victory over Collingwood in round three. The Magpies kicked nine goals to three in a devastating third quarter to take a 30-point lead into the final break, but Chris Scott's seasoned professionals gradually wore down their opponents. With seven unanswered goals in the last term, the Cats prevailed by 13 points with Cameron's six majors his best output since round eight, 2021. Scott said of his team after the game: "They believe. It's been a constant trait of our playing group for a long period." It was no surprise on Brownlow Medal night that Cameron (pictured here celebrating) received the three votes, the first of five occasions throughout 2022. He ended up with 19 votes, was the game's leading forward and finished equal eighth in the medal voting.

CAPTAINCY RECORD: Following Geelong's comeback victory over Collingwood in round three, players from both teams formed a guard of honour to applaud the durable Cats skipper Joel Selwood, who passed former Carlton champion Stephen Kernahan's record for most games as a VFL/AFL captain. Having replaced Cameron Ling as Geelong's leader for the 2012 season—at just 23 years of age—Selwood had now led the Cats in 227 matches, during which time he was named the AFLPA's best captain (2013), led Australia's International Rules team (2014), and was picked as skipper of the 2013-14 and 2016 All-Australian sides. "Joel didn't want it to be all about him, but it's hard [in that situation because] it's a record that's very, very hard to achieve and will be very, very hard to chase down," coach Chris Scott said after the game. "So, it was a significant milestone and one we should recognise. Great for our fans, too."

Ford
GEELONG
CATS

OLD ENEMY: In the now traditional Easter Monday clash against Hawthorn at the MCG, the Cats trailed at half-time before a third-quarter fightback saw them take a two-goal lead at the final change. Given what we've come to expect from these two proud clubs, it came as no surprise that Hawthorn was able to mount a late rally to get home by 12 points in an upset. Tom Hawkins, Jeremy Cameron and Tyson Stengle each kicked three goals, and Isaac Smith (pictured holding off Hawks premiership teammate Luke Breust) gathered 23 disposals and had eight inside-50s against his old club. After five rounds, the Cats were precariously placed in seventh position, already two games behind the unbeaten reigning premier, Melbourne.

AFL
SHERRIN
AFL

KITTENS. With the club often under fire regarding its ageing list, the selectors introduced two newcomers to the side for the round eight clash against the struggling GWS Giants, at Manuka Oval in Canberra. Cooper Stephens (left) and Mitch Knevitt justified their inclusions, gathering 19 and 15 disposals respectively as the Cats controlled the game to win by 53 points. Jeremy Cameron top-scored with five goals against his old club and Tyson Stengle snagged another three, while Mitch Duncan had 33 disposals. But it was Mark Blicavs who would be awarded the three Brownlow Medal votes for his 25 disposals, 21 hit-outs, eight tackles, eight clearances and six inside-50s, highlighting the remarkable versatility the former distance runner brings to the Geelong side.

COTTON:ON
AFL
COTTON:ON
AFL
Ford
GMHBA
GMHBA

HERITAGE AND CULTURE: The annual Sir Doug Nicholls Round has become one of the most popular and emotive celebrations on the AFL calendar. Geelong's Indigenous guernsey for 2022, modelled here by Brandan Parfitt (one of three Indigenous players on Geelong's 2022 list, along with Tyson Stengle and Quinton Narkle), was created by Wadawurrung country's Corrina Eccles and is titled 'Kardiniyoo'. Geelong's home ground, Kardinia Park (now known as GMHBA Stadium), is a place well-known to Wadawurrung people as Kardiniyoo, meaning 'sunrise'.

THAT MAKES THREE!: Leading into round 10, Jake Kolodjashnij had enjoyed a fine 142-game career at the Cattery largely spent defending his team's goal, and it was a rare occurrence—in round 10—to see his name on the scoresheet. For just the third time, he experienced the joy that champion forwards Tom Hawkins and Jeremy Cameron take for granted on a weekly basis. Kolodjashnij drifted forward to kick a goal, then celebrated with teammate and fellow defender Jed Bews (pictured) as the Cats turned out a strong second half to defeat Port Adelaide, at GMHBA Stadium, by 35 points. It was just his second goal for the season and third for his career.

MR RELIABLE: Although the Cats were below their best against Adelaide in round 11, they had too much class for the rebuilding Crows, winning comfortably by 42 points at GMHBA Stadium. Having missed the presence of star defender Tom Stewart late in 2021 because of a foot injury, a pleasing sign for the Cats was the way he had recovered to once again be picking off opposition forward forays with his usual grace and ease. Against the Crows, Stewart received three Brownlow Medal votes, the second time in the first 11 rounds the umpires had named him the best player afield. Stewart (here marking in front of teammate Brandan Parfitt and Adelaide's Ned McHenry) had 34 kicks and six handballs, took 16 marks and logged 10 rebound-50s, the second time in 2022 that Stewart collected 40 disposals in a match, having also achieved the rare feat against Fremantle in round seven—the only other occasion he was awarded three Brownlow votes in 2022.

COTTON:ON
Ford
AFL
AFL
COTTON:ON
AFL
COTTON:ON

CLEAN PAIR OF HEELS: Sam Menegola, seen here escaping the clutches of West Coast's Tom Barrass during the Cats' 18-point win at Optus Stadium in round 14, endured an interrupted start to 2022, left knee surgery keeping him on the sidelines for the first half of the season. Looking to make up for lost time, Menegola celebrated his first game back, kicking two goals from 20 touches and earning two Brownlow Medal votes. Concussion forced him to miss rounds 19 and 20 and then soreness kept him out the side in the final home and away round, and he was unable to reclaim his place in the finals. After the Grand Final, coach Chris Scott paid tribute to Menegola (named as a Grand Final emergency along with Jonathon Ceglar) and others including Max Holmes; players, he said, who had previously been automatic selections and were desperately unlucky not to play. "For Max, I just feel desperately. That's extended to Sam Menegola, who is just one of the great people you'll meet in footy," he said.

COTTON:ON

MILESTONE MAN. Jeremy Cameron is applauded by teammates as he is chaired off the ground by Tom Hawkins and Brad Close after his 200th AFL match (after 171 with GWS GIANTS). In a thrilling round 15 blockbuster encounter against Richmond at the MCG, Cameron kicked three goals, the last of those restoring the lead for the Cats midway through the final term. But Cameron's influence went far beyond his goalkicking. He attended four centre bounces, helping set up several other goals when the game was on the line. Geelong held on to win by three points, making Cameron's milestone game even sweeter. Coach Chris Scott praised his efforts away from the front half after the match. "He certainly had an impact up the ground," Scott said. "I think we've got some good between-the-arcs ball users, but I haven't seen many better than him." Cameron's three goals took his career tally to 508, which had swelled to 531 by season's end. Only four others—teammate Tom Hawkins, Sydney's Lance Franklin, Eagle Josh Kennedy and Richmond's Jack Riewoldt—have registered more goals in the time since Cameron's AFL debut in 2012.

Ford
AFL
COTTON:ON

SPIRIT OF TASMANIA

A LOW-FLYING 'HAWK': Geelong's round 16 victory over North Melbourne was a demolition job. On a cold winter's night, the Cats ran hot at GMHBA Stadium after an even first quarter to blow the Kangaroos away. The final winning margin of 112 points was Geelong's biggest since 2018 and the final score of 21.18 (144) was the Cats' highest of the season. Tom Hawkins (here at full stretch marking in front of North's Josh Walker) booted six of his side's 21 goals, his biggest haul since his half dozen against Essendon at the same venue almost a year ago.

MITCH'S NIGHT OUT: It might have been his 250th AFL match, but veteran Mitch Duncan's performance in Geelong's round 16 dismantling of North Melbourne showed there's plenty of life left in the old boy yet. Duncan (seen here on the shoulders of teammates Joel Selwood and Tom Hawkins) had 30 disposals and took 14 marks in a masterful display, which came 22 days after his 31st birthday. In a post-match interview, Duncan was typically humble: "I feel so privileged to land where I did. We play in such big games [and] we have such good people at the footy club." Duncan's first captain Cameron Ling said the East Perth product had a strong work ethic and commitment to improvement from the moment he was drafted in 2009. "He was there to learn, he was there to get better and contribute in a big way," Ling said before Duncan's milestone match. "He's one of our most crucial players."

COTTON:ON
AFL
Ford
Ford
Ford
COTTON:ON

FIXATED: Jed Bews's nine disposals in the round 16 win over North Melbourne was a modest total by his standards but was easily explained. Such was Geelong's dominance on the night, the ball lived in the Cats' forward line for much of the evening, giving Bews and his defensive-half teammates a less challenging job than normal.

TOP OF THE TABLE: Geelong's Thursday night round 17 encounter with reigning premier Melbourne was a second versus first affair; the Cats looking to knock the Demons off their perch and claim top place. The game was an arm-wrestle for three quarters, befitting of a clash between two AFL powerhouses, and Geelong's lead was still only five points midway through the final term. That's when Cameron Guthrie got significantly involved. His second goal of the match at the 19-minute mark was the first of a run of three that saw the Cats storm away to a 28-point win and claim ladder leadership. Guthrie (here being hugged by teammate Brad Close after kicking a goal) had 28 touches to go with his two goals and received two Brownlow Medal votes. Geelong was never again headed on the ladder and Guthrie would go on to win his second 'Carji' Greeves Medal (in a tie with Jeremy Cameron) in the count on the Thursday night after the Grand Final.

A FAMILY AFFAIR: Geelong's Sam De Koning and his brother Tom share a moment after Geelong's 30-point win over Carlton at the MCG in round 18. The pair's father Terry De Koning played 31 games for Footscray in the early 1980s, not enough for his sons to be drafted to the Dogs via the father-son rule (100 senior games required for eligibility). Sam, 18 months younger than Tom, played all but two AFL games for the Cats in 2022 after just one in his first two seasons after he was a first-round draft choice in 2019 (pick 19). After the match coach Chris Scott described Sam as an "overnight success that took three years". Scott explained further: "The current idea in the AFL is that if you're a young player you should walk into a team and get opportunities straight away. The great Geelong players of a decade ago didn't get that luxury. We thought it appropriate that Sam got some experience in different parts of the ground so that when he came in, he was really prepared."

COTTON ON
Ford
GEELONG
CATS

MATCHING PAIR: Gryan Miers and Max Holmes were key contributors in Geelong's 10-goal defeat of the Gold Coast Suns at Metricon Stadium in round 22. They each kicked two goals as the Cats dominated the match, particularly in the first half. Between them, the pair kicked the last two goals of the second quarter—Geelong's 11th and 12th—to give the Cats a 51-point lead at the long break. They kicked another major each as the Cats cruised to victory. Holmes was 16 days shy of his 20th birthday on this night, but his excellent performance belied the fact he was a teenager playing in just his 24th AFL match. The son of former Olympic sprinter Lee Naylor shows plenty of pace of his own, excelling on a wing.

COTTON:ON
AFL
Ford
GEELONG CATS
AFL
COTTON:ON

SHERRIN
AFL
GMHBa

▲ **ALL CLASS AND ALL-AUSTRALIAN:** Ahead of their finals campaign, five Cats achieved All-Australian selection, with Tom Hawkins, receiving a blazer for a fifth time, named captain. Despite missing five matches, Tom Stewart earned a fourth spot in his sixth season, while Jeremy Cameron collected his third blazer, his previous two coming as a Giant in 2013 and 2019. Mark Blicavs and Tyson Stengle were named for the first time. Given he is not even Geelong's captain, Hawkins's selection as skipper came as a surprise, even to him. "I don't think I've actually ever been captain of a football side, so to be standing alongside some of the best players of our generation is pretty cool," he said. Fellow All-Australian and ex-Richmond teammate Shai Bolton couldn't hide his delight at the selection of Stengle, who a year earlier had been plying his trade at state league-level in South Australia. "It's probably one of the biggest stories in the AFL to be honest," said Bolton. "I'm super proud of him and how he's played football."

2022 ALL-AUSTRALIAN TEAM
BACK ROW (FROM LEFT): Isaac Heeney (Sydney Swans), Mark Blicavs (Geelong), Sam Taylor (GWS Giants), Max Gawn (Melbourne), Charlie Curnow (Carlton), Andrew Brayshaw (Fremantle), Tom Stewart (Geelong).
MIDDLE ROW: Jack Sinclair (St Kilda), Callum Mills (Sydney Swans), Jeremy Cameron (Geelong), Brayden Maynard (Collingwood), Steven May (Melbourne), Christian Petracca (Melbourne), Clayton Oliver (Melbourne), Lachie Neale (Brisbane Lions).
FRONT ROW: Touk Miller (Gold Coast Suns), Adam Saad (Carlton), Patrick Cripps (Carlton, vice-captain), Tom Hawkins (Geelong, captain), Connor Rozee (Port Adelaide), Shai Bolton (Richmond), Tyson Stengle (Geelong).

◀ **ALL-ROUNDER:** It might have been Patrick Dangerfield's 300th match, but Mark Blicavs almost stole the limelight from 'Danger' with a commanding performance against West Coast in round 23. Sharing ruck duties with Jonathon Ceglar, Blicavs had 16 hit-outs and 25 touches and also laid four tackles, his efforts later rewarded with three Brownlow Medal votes. Even after more than 200 AFL matches, Blicavs is often characterised as an athlete rather than what he has proven to be—a genuine star footballer. "He's just a really important player for us," coach Chris Scott said during the season. "[The word is] often misused in AFL, but he's unique. There's no one else like him."

A SEPTEMBER TO SAVOUR

As Geelong embarked on its 2022 finals campaign, Chris Scott had practically a full list to choose from. Crucially, defender Tom Stewart had overcome a serious foot injury that kept him out of the 2021 finals campaign and was back to All-Australian form, and forward Jeremy Cameron was at his peak after a fractured 2021 season.

In the forced week's break between the last home and away round and the first week of finals, which the AFL had first introduced in 2016, five Cats were selected in the All-Australian side—Stewart, Cameron, Mark Blicavs, Tom Hawkins (named captain) and Tyson Stengle—highlighting the skill, consistency and across-field power of Geelong's team. Young defender Sam De Koning also finished second in voting for the NAB Rising Star. But despite Geelong's dominance in the second half of the season, the fairytale story throughout 2022 had been first-year coach Craig McCrae's Collingwood—Geelong's opponent in week one of the finals.

The Magpies under McCrae had continually defied the odds to win a record 11 games by under two goals, and seven by six points or less, giving Collingwood supporters hope that their own 12-year Premiership drought was about to end. On a Saturday night in finals-starved Melbourne, 91,525 spectators all but filled the MCG to witness one of the great finals. Scott's finals record in the first week since 2011's dominance had been disappointing, with just three wins from 10 appearances, but on this night his finals-hardened men took the best their opponents could throw at them and, in the dying moments—led by a last-term cameo from Gary Rohan and a late goal to Max Holmes—won the pulsating tug of war by six points.

With one hoodoo eliminated, it was on to the Preliminary Final; another obstacle the Cats had struggled to overcome, winning just one of six since the 2011 campaign. Their opponent, the Brisbane Lions, had sent reigning Premier Melbourne packing in an impressive semi-final performance, and suddenly there was a groundswell of support for Chris Fagan's team—which also had had its share of finals heartbreak in recent seasons—to add to Geelong's finals misery. But it didn't take long for the new-look Cats to stamp their authority on a match in which they had Brisbane's measure from go to whoa. A 14-point lead at the first break became 30 points at the half, before the Cats turned on a third quarter to remember. They piled on 7.4 to just 2.1, putting the result beyond doubt as they cruised away to win by 71 points—a rare blowout in what had been an otherwise captivating and highly competitive finals series. Hawkins kicked four goals, Stengle three, while Patrick Dangerfield, Blicavs and Mitch Duncan dominated around the ground.

But a perfect night was soured late when Max Holmes, a gut-running link-up man all season, injured a hamstring. He would spend the week working feverishly to defy the odds and prove his fitness for the Grand Final. At first, he was out of the side, then he was in but by Grand Final eve, Scott made the brutal call of replacing him with medical substitute Mark O'Connor. Holmes was the heartbreak story of an otherwise magical month for the club, but he was there on the sidelines during the Grand Final, cheering his teammates home against the Sydney Swans. Geelong's one-in, all-in culture of support was there for all to see through Holmes's positive attitude.

For all bar Geelong players, staff and supporters, the Grand Final failed to live up to the hype, with Sydney never in the hunt against a team prepared to stop at nothing in pursuit of the Premiership. Typifying this approach was Dangerfield (later awarded the Gary Ayres Medal as best player in the finals series) who finally got to grab a Premiership medallion in his second Grand Final. The suspicion was that this might be Joel Selwood's grand finale, from the moment he snapped a brilliant goal in the final quarter and was swamped by his teammates. Four days later, he confirmed the guesswork, retiring as a living legend of the football club. Geelong has now won 10 VFL/AFL Premierships, with Selwood the club's only four-time winner. **G**

Dan Eddy

HERE WE GO AGAIN: For the fourth successive season, and the ninth time during Chris Scott's remarkably successful 12-season reign as coach, Geelong finished in the top four and earned a double chance in the finals. However, with an underwhelming 1-8 record in the first week of finals, Scott knew his Cats needed to be at their very best against the resurgent Collingwood in the first Qualifying Final to give their 2022 campaign the perfect start.

TOYOTA
TOYOTA
TOYOTA
TOYOTA
TOYOTA
TOYOTA
TOYOTA
TOYOTA
TOYOTA
TOYOTA
TOYOTA
SPORTCREATIVE
THEOREM
SWEET
Vinidex
Vinidex
GEORGIE
GEORGIE
NO VAPING. EVICTIONS WILL OCCUR.
DAIMLER TRUCK
18:17
4 9 33
4 · 9 · 33
13:58
AFL

SATURDAY TWILIGHT: The MCG provided the perfect backdrop to one of the all-time great finals when Geelong met Collingwood in the first Qualifying Final. It was the 26th final between two of the inaugural VFL clubs since their first in 1897, in the competition's first season. A remarkable crowd of 91,525 spectators filled Melbourne's mighty coliseum to witness a seesawing, edge-of-the-seat contest that remained in the balance until the final seconds. Here, Zach Tuohy gets his kick away despite the close checking of Magpie Jack Crisp, as Jeremy Cameron and Jeremy Howe watch on.

AFL
GMHBA

▲ **OUCH:** A late lunge from the Collingwood ruckman Mason Cox might have caused him an earache, but doesn't stop Tom Atkins getting the ball clear for another Geelong forward thrust.

◀ **ELITE STOPPER:** Having missed Geelong's 2021 finals campaign with a serious Lisfranc injury in his left foot, Tom Stewart returned to his best in 2022 and had a major say in the Cats producing the third-tightest defence of the home-and-away season (1488 points against, an average of 67.6 points per game [behind Melbourne, 1483 and Fremantle, 1486]). It wasn't all smooth sailing for Stewart however, when he copped a four-match suspension for striking Richmond's Dion Prestia late in the season, an uncharacteristic action that threatened to impact Geelong's Premiership ambitions. After the Grand Final, Stewart owned up to the misdemeanour. "That was one of the hardest moments of my football career, to be honest with you," he told the Herald Sun. "I tried to own my actions—I had to. The few days after the incident were seriously tough. A lot of people judged me on that one action, and it was extremely difficult, but ultimately, I did do the wrong thing. I try to be the best version of myself every day. Hopefully, I don't get remembered for that." Fortunately, by September, Stewart was back patrolling Geelong's defensive half, earning a fourth All-Australian jacket before gathering 22 disposals and taking seven marks in the Qualifying Final victory over Collingwood.

ALL SHAPES AND SIZES: Despite their vastly different backgrounds, Collingwood's Mason Cox (who grew up in the United States playing basketball) and Geelong's Mark Blicavs (a former steeplechaser) faced off in this ruck contest, each playing critical roles for their respective teams. At 211cm, Cox acts as a lightning rod for his smaller Collingwood teammates, who rely on his palming of the ball to generate attacking forays. Blicavs, at 198cm and 100kg, defies logic with his ability to utilise his unparalleled endurance to 'break the lines', effectively acting as an extra midfielder, to tag, to take on the ruck or to become a key defender. His versatility is unique in the modern game. He played his part in the win, with eight hit-outs and three clearances.

LIMPING CAT: A scare went through the Geelong camp in the second quarter when rebounding defender Jake Kolodjashnij suffered a tibiofibular joint injury to his right knee. Initially, Kolodjashnij made a brave return to the field before medical staff erred on the side of caution and subbed him out of the game. Kolodjashnij, whose parents emigrated to Tasmania from Soviet-ruled Ukraine after World War II, was replaced before half-time by the Irish-born Mark O'Connor. When the Cats defeated the Magpies and earned a week's rest, Kolodjashnij's chances of being fit for the Preliminary Final increased, but he faced a race against time to prove he had recovered sufficiently.

I CAN'T HEAR YOU: Geelong's latest superstar in the No.5 guernsey—following on from club greats, Graham 'Polly' Farmer and Gary Ablett Snr—Jeremy Cameron kicked three important goals, happily engaging with a typically opinionated Collingwood cheer squad during the nailbiting Qualifying Final. A laidback country lad, Cameron has slotted into the Cats forward line seamlessly; his hard running, ability to find space, clever left foot, powerful marking and canny game sense, make him one of the most valuable players in the game. As Cameron enjoyed his exchange with the crowd, some of his opponents were left wondering what more they could have done to stop him. The most disappointed Magpie of all, at least at this moment, was defender Brayden Maynard, seen here looking to the heavens for answers. When the game was done, media commentators rated Cameron as the most important player in the final; remarkably, he would receive just one vote from the two coaches.

HEARTFELT: Having arrived at Geelong from Carlton after the 2016 season, hard-nut defender Zach Tuohy was quickly embraced by the Geelong faithful. In turn, the energetic and courageous Tuohy was soon at home in the blue and white hoops. Against the Magpies, Tuohy was playing his 248th League game (128th for Geelong). Always one to wear his heart on his sleeve (and a catalogue of tattoos on his arms and legs), Tuohy is one of the game's most animated celebrators.

MATCH-WINNER: Despite having his share of critics for previous moderate performances in finals, Geelong half-forward Gary Rohan elevated his game to greater heights in the victory over Collingwood. When the Cats required a hero, up jumped Rohan to take this superb pack mark late in the final term. Former Western Bulldogs champion Luke Darcy, commentating for Channel 7, was in awe as he described the moment: "He marked it like (North Melbourne great) Wayne Carey," he said, as Geelong fans erupted. The former Sydney Swan, in his 69th game for the Cats, then went back and thumped the Sherrin home from just outside 50 at the city end of the ground to put his team narrowly in front, setting the stage for a thrilling finish. Rohan led the coaches' voting for the match with nine votes.

Ford
9
AFL

TO THE MAX: When Collingwood's running midfielder Jack Crisp levelled the scores at 72 points each, the pulsating match appeared headed for extra time. Enter 20-year-old Max Holmes, who capped a tremendous season with the game-winning goal to send the Cats into a Preliminary Final. As his teammates willed the ball from defence to attack along the Shane Warne Stand wing, Holmes took off, unattended through the middle of the MCG, in an endeavour to provide a scoring option in the forward half. Jeremy Cameron's long kick dramatically slipped through the hands of Gary Rohan, who quickly recovered and, while horizontal, handballed to Holmes as he ran into the open goal. Holmes's goal sent Cats supporters into raptures while simultaneously breaking Magpie hearts. In a cruel twist, a fortnight later, Holmes would later see his season end in heartbreak.

THUMBS UP: In his 24th final, 31-year-old West Australian-born midfielder Mitch Duncan was yet again one of Geelong's best contributors in a big game. Duncan, all smiles here with ruckman Rhys Stanley, had 23 disposals, took five marks and kicked a goal in the Cats' six-point victory. He was just one win away from a third Grand Final appearance and a crack at a second Premiership, having won his first in 2011, against Collingwood.

I'VE GOT YOUR BACK, GAZ: Geelong coach Chris Scott knew as well as anyone the criticism Gary Rohan had endured for previous below par performances in finals. That was why Scott made a beeline for his red-headed half-forward following the team's six-point victory over Collingwood, offering his congratulations for Rohan's last-quarter heroics that catapulted the Cats into a Preliminary Final. In the post-game press conference, Scott—who had admitted on Channel 9's *Footy Classified* pre-finals program: "I get a bit defensive of my players and I wear that as a badge of honour"—reaffirmed that thinking after the victory, praising Rohan's role and his impact at the club: "Look, it is gratifying, I don't mind saying that. We are really clear on what he can bring to our team and the way we play. He's absolutely an energy giver, his teammates love playing with him and I'm just really proud of him."

PRIDE IN THE GUERNSEY: Joel Selwood points to his Geelong jumper as he gives his players a rev-up before the Cats' first Preliminary Final encounter with the Brisbane Lions at the MCG. The skipper (surrounded here by Zach Guthrie, Patrick Dangerfield and Brad Close) was keen for his players to exorcise any perceived demons resulting from a decade of failed finals campaigns, including losses in five of six Preliminary Finals since their 2011 Premiership. The Preliminary Final victory would become Selwood's 21st win in a final, with the Grand Final a week later making it 22. To give context to the magnitude of that achievement, Selwood's wins are equal to the number of finals the St Kilda club has won in 126 League seasons!

COTTON:ON
AFL
Ford
COTTON:ON
AFL
Ford
GMHBA

ALL SMILES: Geelong coach Chris Scott and his Brisbane counterpart Chris Fagan share a lighter moment before the Preliminary Final. Only one of them would be smiling by night's end. It was Scott, who would lead his team to the third Grand Final of his 12-season tenure. The Preliminary Final, his eighth as Geelong's coach, was Scott's 500th AFL match—215 as a player with the Brisbane Lions and 285 coaching the Cats. It was also his 27th final as a coach after 16 playing with the Lions.

FULL FOCUS: Rhys Stanley's focus on the ball is typically intense as he sends the Cats into attack. Since crossing to Geelong from St Kilda (2010-2014, 58 games) Stanley has endured occasional criticism for inconsistency during his eight seasons at Kardinia Park, but his team-focused acts often go unseen and unheralded. Against Brisbane in the Preliminary Final, he recorded five 'one-percenters' (knock-ons, spoils, smothers or shepherds), matched only by Patrick Dangerfield. Stanley also laid three tackles, had 18 hit-outs and five of his nine possessions were contested, underlining his value to the team.

100% ACTION: Since making his AFL debut in round two of the 2018 season, Jack Henry has not put a foot wrong as an intercepting defender, and he played that role to perfection against the Lions. In the first half when the match was up for grabs, Henry and his defensive-half teammates intercepted the ball 13 times, strangling the Brisbane forward line. Henry was the only player on either side to spend the entire match on the field, his 100 per cent game time yielding nine marks. Along with Tom Stewart, Jake Kolodjashnij and Sam De Koning, the Geelong defenders turned back countless Brisbane forays, restricting the Lions to 7.7 (49), their lowest score of the year.

OUT OF THE SHADOWS: Zach Guthrie might not have had as many possessions (19) as his more highly feted big brother Cam (21) in Geelong's Preliminary Final win, but his other stats suggest he made up that narrow deficit in other ways. Zach laid seven tackles, had four defensive rebounds and kicked the last goal of the match, demonstrating he has well and truly emerged from his sibling's shadow. The Preliminary Final was the younger Guthrie's 53rd AFL match but, perhaps more importantly, his 17th in a row, after he had established his credentials in 2021 playing 13 matches including Geelong's two finals.

Ford

SHOWDOWN: Patrick Dangerfield musters all his strength to escape the clutches of Brisbane's Lachie Neale. Both are past winners of the Brownlow Medal, (Dangerfield in 2016 and Neale in 2020), but on this night it was Dangerfield who took another step towards achieving football's ultimate goal, winning a Premiership medallion. Neale, team-tagged throughout, was well held, along with most of his teammates, but Dangerfield played a starring role in the comfortable win, his 28-touch, two-goal effort earning him the maximum 10 votes from the coaches, with Gryan Miers picking up 8, Tom Hawkins 5, Jake Kolodjashnij 3, and Tom Stewart 2. Brisbane's only vote-getter was Darcy Gardiner (one vote) indicating Geelong's domination across all lines.

MR CONSISTENT: Cam Guthrie, the hard-headed midfielder from Sunbury in Melbourne's north-west, put in a typically solid performance in the Cats' demolition of Brisbane. It is perhaps his consistently high level that sees Guthrie go unnoticed at times, and sometimes unheralded outside Geelong. His elite endurance, toughness and decision-making, along with his clean hand and foot skills were on full display against the Lions. At 30, Guthrie could now be included in Geelong's list of elder statesman at the Cattery, although nine of his teammates in the Preliminary Final victory were older. In the Preliminary Final, the average age of the 23 who took the field was 28 years and 129 days with that average to be bypassed in the Grand Final by another 77 days!

DID THE JOB: Tom Atkins was one of several players charged with putting the clamps on Brisbane's midfield star Lachie Neale in the Preliminary Final. Along with Joel Selwood (and occasionally Mark Blicavs) Atkins did exactly that, restricting the normally prolific Brisbane ball-winner to just 20 touches, his second-lowest total of the year. Given Neale's usual effectiveness with the ball, the tag team's efforts went a long way to setting up the Cats' commanding performance. For Atkins, it was yet another stellar effort from the former lockdown forward and rebound defender, who thrived in his new midfield role in 2022.

A CRUEL BLOW: After many Premiership triumphs there can also be individual heartbreak. Such was the case for Max Holmes, seen here slamming his palms into the MCG boundary turf in frustration late in the Preliminary Final. Holmes had just suffered a strain to his right hamstring, which meant he would almost certainly miss the Grand Final. By the following day, Holmes had picked himself up and was working hard on his rehabilitation, hoping against hope that he could defy the odds and be fit for his maiden AFL Grand Final after 18 games in 2022. The speedy midfielder would not find out his fate until the eve of the game, with the Cats deciding that the risk of including him was not worth taking. Holmes would be named in the team, but Mark O'Connor would take his place after a game-day decision, with Brandan Parfitt becoming the medical sub.

AFL

RAPID RISE: Tyson Stengle can't hide his delight after kicking one of his three goals against Brisbane. Stengle had been kept quiet in the Cats' narrow Qualifying Final win over Collingwood at the MCG a fortnight earlier, but his performance in the Preliminary Final showed why he had made the All-Australian team. His three goals took his season tally to 49, leaving him just one short of becoming the third Cat in 2022 (after Tom Hawkins and Jeremy Cameron) to boot at least 50. Stengle, who had not missed a game for the Cats since making his debut for the club in round one, was also at the top of his defensive game against the Lions, laying four tackles to ensure the ball did not easily escape Geelong's forward area.

BEW-TY: For Jed Bews, the Cats' 71-point win over Brisbane in the Preliminary Final was a great way to celebrate his 150th game, and it was perhaps even greater than even he might have realised. When Jed's father Andrew Bews, who represented both Geelong and Brisbane, played his own 150th game for the Cats in 1990, it was in a 71-point win over Brisbane! While Bews Snr celebrated his milestone match with 34 possessions, four goals and three Brownlow Medal votes, the younger Bews, a small defender who knows how to keep his opponents at bay, while also having a knack for starting many an attack, with 10 disposals, would play his part in Geelong's impassable defensive team within a team. After the smashing win over the Lions, he was given an armchair ride from Jake Kolodjashnij and Mark Blicavs.

DOUBLE HIGH-FIVE!: Tom Atkins and Isaac Smith celebrate after the final siren to put an exclamation mark on Geelong's dominant win over the Lions. For Atkins, the victory meant he would be playing in his first AFL Grand Final. For Smith, it would be a fifth appearance in the decider, the first four of those as a Hawthorn player. First or fifth, it didn't matter—the level of excitement and anticipation was the same for both. Smith had a quiet night by his lofty standards, but with a Premiership at stake, he would take his game to a new level a week later.

SIMPLY DOMINANT

If the AFL Grand Final parade (revamped to include a novel water-borne component on the murky Yarra River) had elicited much mirth and bemusement from some Geelong players, the team was strictly business when it assembled at the MCG the following day. On a glorious spring afternoon and in front of a full house for the first Grand Final at the venue since 2019, the Cats were ready for anything the Swans might conjure in the maiden Grand Final meeting between two clubs that were part of eight that seceded to form the VFL at the end of 1896.

Not long before the opening bounce, Robbie Williams and Delta Goodrem had sent off sparks with an electric finale to the pre-game show, rightly receiving 'hard act to follow' accolades. But the Cats weren't content playing in their shadows, and quickly made some noise of their own, ferociously attacking their opponents and the ball, and moving forward with speed, precision and intent. When they had to defend, they did so stoutly and cleverly, often finding ways to immediately set up counterattacks. With a quarter in the books and its highest first-term return in its 19 Grand Finals (6.5), with the 35-point margin the greatest since 1989, Geelong looked home, a dangerous and reckless idea in today's game, where the 6-6-6 rule in part allows for trailing teams to quickly bridge big gaps. There was, however, enough forensic evidence to suggest the patterns of the game had been established. In what Channel 7's Brian Taylor dubbed "an avalanche of attack" initiated by Tom Hawkins' opening two goals, via his signature work at stoppages, the Cats had registered 20 inside-50s to eight, taken 35 marks to 13 (and five to zero inside 50), dominated contested possession 48-29, and had more than doubled the Swans for time in possession. The stats were simply confirming what our eyes were telling us—the men in blue and white, so often dubbed too old and too slow, were stronger faster, and more aggressive in seeking to 'win' territory. And, 6-6-6 be damned; the contest was over.

"It's gratifying as a coaching group when you spend so much time talking about different 'what-ifs' and trying to set the game up so we could play our style of footy," coach Chris Scott said after the win. "With the quality of the opposition these days, if the game's played their way, you're in trouble. We got the matchups we wanted [and] we got the look of the game that we wanted early, which I suspect gave our players some confidence. It's nice when you go out saying, 'This is what it will look like if we have the game on our terms'. Pretty early on that's how it appeared to us."

With the Swans steadying somewhat in the second term and managing to break even on the scoreboard, some might have believed a turnaround in the second half was a possibility. But quick goals by Mitch Duncan and Brad Close early in the third quarter sent the Swans into territory frequented by the novelist Franz Kafka: "Oh, there is hope, an infinite amount of hope ... but not for us."

The Cats' six goals to nil mirrored their first-quarter effort, with the now 74-point margin at the last change giving them a chance to best their greatest winning Grand Final margin of 119 points set in 2007, especially given a gentle reminder from captain Joel Selwood, to play out the game as they have played the season; show no mercy.

Some cheek from the Swans ensured any quest for a new record margin would be snuffed. But there was still time for a memorable finish—at least for Geelong—and for a set of exclamation marks on a wonderful season that culminated with the ultimate team effort in the Grand Final. After so many seasons when the Cats had dominated through the season, but couldn't get it done in the end, this victory erased all those memories, all those queries. **G**

Peter Di Sisto

ALL ABOARD: In a break from tradition, the AFL added a new component to the annual Grand Final Parade, kick-starting the popular event on the murky waters of Melbourne's Yarra River. The Geelong and Sydney teams boarded separate boats to ferry them from the Swan Street Bridge to Princes Bridge, then back to Birrarung Marr, where they would disembark to complete the final leg of the journey to Yarra Park, outside the MCG, now on the back of Toyota HiLux utes. Although the likes of Geelong coach Chris Scott and skipper Joel Selwood in their coach-captain speedboat, saw the funny side, many supporters were left disappointed at being unable to see their heroes as intimately as in previous years. Even the Prime Minister Anthony Albanese had an opinion on the format, joking to outgoing AFL CEO Gillon McLachlan, at the North Melbourne Breakfast the next day: "To Gill, I would say, having watched the parade on the Yarra yesterday, to quote a former Prime Minister, 'We do need to stop the boats.'"

ROBBIE ROCKS THE 'G: From the moment British rock star Robbie Williams emerged, atop a rising podium to begin his pre-game performance, and declaring "I'm going to be phenomenal, so you'd better be good", perceived Grand Final entertainment blunders of the past were forgotten. For 20 minutes, Williams rocked the 'G in the type of high-octane show Grand Final crowds have rarely seen. If he hadn't already won over Australian audiences, his tributes to the late cricket legend Shane Warne and local music icon John Farnham, currently undergoing treatment for cancer, plus a final duet with our own musical queen Delta Goodrem, would have. The brilliant performance underlined Williams' status as one of the greatest solo acts on the planet.

CATS
GEELONG
CATS
COTTON:ON

THE CAT'S WHISKERS: Having missed their club's previous Grand Final appearance, at the Gabba in Brisbane in 2020, when the global pandemic disrupted so much of 'normal' life and Melbourne and parts of regional Victoria were in strict lockdown, Geelong supporters were not going to miss the chance to cheer their team in the first Grand Final played at the MCG since 2019. And they had plenty to cheer about, as the Cats were on top from start to finish against a disappointing Sydney. A crowd of 100,024 filled the 'G, a record for the AFL era and the highest Grand Final attendance since 1986.

JOEL'S ARMY: Entering the finals cauldron for a record 40th time (and edging past Hawthorn great Michael Tuck's finals mark of 39), Geelong skipper Joel Selwood was on a mission. Having last tasted Premiership glory in 2011, Selwood and his teammates had fallen short in many finals over the ensuing decade. But this hardened team was a different beast and there was nothing, not even a young and dynamic Sydney Swans squad, that was going to stand in its way in their pursuit of a Premiership. Joining Selwood on the march to victory are (from left) Zach Tuohy, Mark Blicavs, Cam Guthrie (partly obscured), Mitch Duncan, Tom Hawkins and Tom Stewart. Selwood, Duncan and Hawkins are the only 'survivors' from that 2011 Grand Final triumph over Collingwood.

COTTON:ON
AFL
GRAND FINAL
2022
Ford
GEELONG
CATS
gmhba
AFL

LITTLE LEVI: Not for the first time, an Ablett stole the show on Grand Final Day. But on this occasion, it wasn't 1989 Norm Smith medallist Gary Ablett Snr, nor his dual Premiership-winning son Gary Ablett Jnr, who dominated the MCG stage. Instead, Levi Ablett, son of Gary Jnr, was centre stage after Geelong captain Joel Selwood carried the smiling three-year-old through the team banner before the game. There was barely a dry eye in the stadium as Levi—who suffers from a rare degenerative disease that means he may never speak—was passed from his dad to 'uncle' Joel, who, in the lead-up to the game, had arranged such a fitting gesture for his former teammate and Levi's mother, Jordan. Selwood gently kissed Levi on the head twice, before and after walking through the banner, before handing him back to Gary, who could be heard saying: "I love you, brother," as he held his son and thanked his great friend. Selwood said after the game: "We were able to make it work, and it was so special. For that family too. They've been unbelievable for the Geelong footy club for so many years, it was just a kind little gesture." Wrote Jordan on social media: "The success of the club is without a doubt built on the backs of the wonderful humans within the four walls. It's a privilege to be part of the Cats family! This was a moment that our family and extended family will cherish forever. Levi being one of the boys on GF day with a 100,000-plus crowd roaring. It was just magic."

COTTON:ON
COTTON:ON
GARY ABLETT
COTTON:ON

GREATEST TEAM OF ALL: The 23 players and the coach just moments before their assault on a 10th Premiership, in Geelong's 19th League Grand Final.

BACK ROW (FROM LEFT): Zach Tuohy, Mitch Duncan, Gary Rohan, Jake Kolodjashnij, Zach Guthrie, Jack Henry, Tom Hawkins, Sam De Koning, Jeremy Cameron, Rhys Stanley, Mark O'Connor, Mark Blicavs, Isaac Smith (still in tracksuit pants!) and Brad Close.
FRONT ROW (FROM LEFT): Brandan Parfitt, Gryan Miers, Tyson Stengle, Jed Bews, Patrick Dangerfield, Chris Scott, Joel Selwood, Tom Stewart, Cam Guthrie and Tom Atkins.

46
Ford
QBE
AFL

HERO TOM: Despite planning for such an event, the Sydney players were unable to nullify Tom Hawkins' trademark move of nudging out his opponent at a forward-half stoppage, plucking the ball from the ruck and snapping a crucial goal. 'Tomahawk's' two memorable first-quarter goals, which kick-started Geelong's charge to glory, both came from boundary throw-ins deep in the forward line. Here, he receives congratulations from teammates Mark Blicavs, Joel Selwood and Gary Rohan. Former Port Adelaide champion Kane Cornes, in his role as a commentator, criticised Swans ruckman Tom Hickey after the game for twice allowing Hawkins to outmanoeuvre him in those crucial contests. But, in Hickey's defence, there are few in the competition who can out-muscle Hawkins when the ball's in his zone. In his 327th appearance in a Geelong guernsey, Hawkins was at his imposing best, with seven score involvements, three goals and nine votes from the coaches.

'BUDDY' QUIET: Sydney superstar Lance 'Buddy' Franklin is always the X-factor the Swans hope can spark their team into action. However, due to the brilliant teamwork and desperation of Geelong's defence, including Jack Henry (here holding Franklin at bay), the 35-year-old Swan was rarely sighted. Franklin booted his 1000th goal against the Cats at the SCG in round two and was expected to be dangerous on the wider expanses of the MCG, but he was given far less swagger room in which to work his magic. He finished the day with just four kicks, one handball, two marks and a solitary behind in Sydney's 8.4 (52) score. Henry told *The Age* after the game: "I played on him when he kicked his 1000th goal and he gave me a bit of a bath. I was a bit rustier earlier in the year—I just needed to get to his body and try my best to beat him in the air." Henry did that, and more. Of Franklin's six Grand Final appearances (2008, 2012, 2013, with Hawthorn, 2014, 2016 and 2022 with Sydney) in his stunning 341-game career, this was the first he has been held goalless in a decider.

COTTON

RECRUITING MASTERCLASS: Long known for astute recruiting coups, the Cats certainly lived up to their reputation when, at the end of the 2020 season, they enticed veterans Jeremy Cameron and Isaac Smith to the club. Cameron, a nine-time leading goalkicker for the GWS GIANTS and a member of the club's first Grand Final team (2019), arrived via a multi-selection trade deal, while Smith, a triple-Premiership Hawthorn wingman (2013–15), found his way to the Cattery as an unrestricted free agent. Both proved critical in Geelong's 2022 Premiership assault. Cameron—in a two-pronged attack with Tom Hawkins—kicked 65 goals in 2022, including two in the Grand Final, while Smith, the Norm Smith medallist, ran amok from start to finish, amassing 32 disposals and kicking three goals, including this one in the opening term as Geelong built a 35-point quarter-time lead that proved a margin too far for the Swans to bridge. In the *Herald Sun*, Smith said of his move to Geelong: "It was about lifestyle and Geelong are a great club and the learnings I have [received] not just about football but [from] the organisation [have] been invaluable. They have been fantastic for us."

COTTON:ON
AFL
GRAND FINAL
2022
Ford
CATS
FOOTBALL CLUB

AFL
SHERRIN
Ford
AFL
COTTON ON

SON OF A GUN: 'Jumping' Jack Hawkins was a favourite of Geelong supporters during his 182-game career at Kardinia Park (1973–81), but the closest he came to experiencing Grand Final day as a player was back-to-back preliminary final appearances in 1980–81, both losses. It took the emergence of his son, Tom, in 2009, to finally break the family drought. That year, Hawkins kicked two goals in Geelong's 12-point Grand Final victory over St Kilda, then, two years later, he was the hero in the Cats' come-from-behind victory against Collingwood, his nine marks and three goals that afternoon almost single-handedly changing the momentum of the match. Eleven years later, as a 34-year-old veteran of the team, Hawkins (here getting a kick away from Tom McCartin) again altered the course of history, with his three goals helping Geelong blow Sydney away in the opening half. It turned out to be a big weekend for the Hawkins family, with Tom's younger brother Charlie also a Premiership winner, with Old Geelong reserves in the VAFA competition.

BLITZING: Mark Blicavs was once a promising steeplechaser and distance runner hell-bent on gaining selection for the Australian Olympic team in the 1500m event. His father Andris played basketball for Australia at the 1976 Montreal Olympics, while his mother Karen qualified for the 1984 Olympic team in basketball but was forced to pull out after injuring her knee two weeks before the team's departure. Mark's sister Sara represented the Opals at the 2020 Tokyo Games, and in the 2022 World Cup campaign in Sydney, and plays for the Southside Flyers in the WNBL, further underlining the remarkable athletic traits that flow through the family genes. When Mark's Olympic dream failed to materialise, his endurance and height made him an attractive prospect for Geelong's recruiters. Since then, he has become one of the most versatile players in the club's history, never more evident than in 2022, when the dual 'Carji' Greeves medallist (2015 and 2018) played in defence and in the midfield. On Grand Final day, he kicked Geelong's third goal to help secure a different type of medal than the one he had earlier dreamed of.

SHOW STOPPER: He didn't register a mention when the votes were submitted to determine the 2022 Norm Smith medallist, but Jake Kolodjashnij was most certainly worthy of a nomination. His negating role on Sydney's potential match-winner Isaac Heeney, (who kicked five goals when the teams met in round two) who was viewed as a key danger man the Cats needed to blanket, was pivotal to Geelong's ultimate success. As usual, Kolodjashnij—who had recovered from a right knee injury suffered in the first Qualifying Final—didn't let the team down. Not only did he collect seven disposals in the first quarter, he also helped keep Heeney without a disposal until early in the second quarter, in what proved a major body blow to Sydney's chances. By day's end, Kolodjashnij had recorded 17 disposals and 11 marks, while Heeney managed just 11 disposalsand one goal in one of his poorest games of the season.

MR CONSISTENT: In a 258-game, 13-year career at the Cattery, Mitch Duncan has been as reliable as worn-in football boots, tirelessly running and providing crucial link-up roles for his team. Having experienced Premiership success in his second season, Duncan—along with 2011 Premiership teammates Joel Selwood and Tom Hawkins—had been forced to wait another 11 years, and 22 finals, to reach the pinnacle. As usual, when the stakes were at their highest, Duncan did what Duncan does best. He had seven disposals in the first term, five in the second, six in the third and, despite the game being well and truly determined by the last quarter, ran and ran some more to add another nine and take his final tally for the day to 27. He also had a game-high 13 marks, plus a sure-to-be-regularly-replayed goal, which came after a desperate tackle on Sydney defender Tom McCartin deep in Geelong's forward line.

THE NEW BREED: Geelong's stellar 2022 season was due to a variety of factors and personnel, one of which was the emergence of Tom Atkins, who, some say, is a clone of his skipper Joel Selwood. In his fourth AFL season, Atkins was a revelation, yet another game-turning hard nut in blue and white hoops. Atkins, renowned for his fearless, no-holds-barred attack on the ball, played all 25 games in 2022, accumulating a career-high 452 disposals, including 23 in the first Qualifying Final victory over Collingwood. Born 12 days before Geelong's 1995 Grand Final loss to Carlton, Atkins missed selection for the 2020 Grand Final defeat by Richmond and, throughout 2022, was as driven as anyone to help the Cats break their 11-year Premiership drought. On Grand Final day, he gathered 16 disposals and had seven tackles—second only to Mark Blicavs in tackles laid for Geelong—to help set the tone for what was to be a memorable afternoon.

CLOSING IN: Having enjoyed Premiership success with SANFL club Glenelg in 2019, Brad Close arrived at Kardinia Park via the 2020 NAB AFL Rookie Draft (pick 14). After eight games but no finals in his first season, Close became a regular member of the team throughout 2021, playing in all three of Geelong's finals, including the 83-point preliminary final thrashing by the eventual Premier, Melbourne. The medium-sized, slick-moving half-forward took his game to another level in 2022, playing all 25 matches and kicking 26 goals, including a career-high four against Sydney at the SCG in round two. When the two teams met again on Grand Final day, Close brought up his first major late in the opening term, then kicked a second goal early in the third quarter when he sensationally intercepted a Tom McCartin kick across goal to send a dagger into the hearts of all Swans supporters. His eight score involvements for the day were two more than any player wearing red and white colours could produce.

LATE CALL-UP: Mark O'Connor was a late inclusion in the side for the Grand Final after Max Holmes was declared unfit after failing to fully recover from a right hamstring injury sustained in the preliminary final. O'Connor (here tacking Sydney's James Rowbottom) was determined to make every post a winner in the big match. He had five disposals in the Cats' dominant first quarter and finished with 13 disposals for the day. He also took six marks to more than justify his inclusion in the starting line-up after spending three of the team's previous four matches as the medical substitute. As the clock wound down in the dying moments of the Grand Final, O'Connor was seen embracing Holmes near the bench, appreciative of the opportunity to play an important role in the victory. O'Connor—one of two Irish-born players in the Geelong side (Zach Tuohy is the other)—explained after the game: "As soon as the final siren went, thoughts went straight to 'Maxy'. I was on the bench at the final siren and Maxy came down and I just gave him a hug. You don't wish that on anyone [missing a Grand Final because of injury], but it's been a squad thing and we have guys that are ready to go and fortunately I got the nod."

A HAIRY MOMENT: In his first season (2011), Cam Guthrie played just two games in Geelong's Premiership run, but in the years since he has gradually developed to be a key component of the team. In 2020, he was named All-Australian, won the 'Carji' Greeves Medal as Geelong's best and fairest, and played in the losing Grand Final against Richmond. He was even more dominant in 2021, amassing a career-high 667 disposals and adding an extra string to Chris Scott's midfield bow, with Joel Selwood, Patrick Dangerfield and Mitch Duncan. Guthrie's 2022 season was equally impressive. He played all 25 games and averaged just under 25 disposals per outing, leading to a second 'Carji'. Although his output was down on Grand Final day (16 disposals), Guthrie's usual grunt work and his iconic flowing locks were on show for all to see, particularly in this shot, as he fights off James Rowbottom while teammate Tom Atkins looks on. Late in the game, he had to leave the field with a right hamstring strain, allowing Brandan Parfitt, the medical sub, to join the festivities.

Ford

AFL
2022

MY SPACE: Patrick Dangerfield finds himself clear of traffic as he sends the Cats forward. This was one of 14 kicks Dangerfield had on the day, to go with his 13 handballs. His 27 touches and bullocking work all over the ground earned him 10 Norm Smith Medal votes, behind only Isaac Smith (14). One member of the voting panel, though, Jonathan Brown—the former Brisbane Lions captain who knows a thing or two about winning Grand Finals—rated Dangerfield the best player on the ground. The coaches agreed with the Norm Smith panel, naming Smith as best afield with 15 votes, from Dangerfield (12) and Tom Hawkins (9).

DEFENCE MEETS ATTACK: Defender Jed Bews and small forward Tyson Stengle celebrate Stengle's goal early in the second term. Having jumped out to a 35-point lead by quarter-time, the Cats were keen to ensure they carried momentum into the second quarter. Stengle's major, which came within the first five minutes, did just that. It was his first of the match and 50th of the season. Stengle added another later in the quarter and two more in the third term.

Ford
GEELONG
CATS

LENDING A HAND: Zach Guthrie, here dishing off a handball to set up play, is no longer as green a footballer as his boots, worn so his grandmother can easily spot him when she's watching on television! Once seen more as a handy back-up for the Cats, Guthrie this season entrenched himself in Geelong's best 22 long before Grand Final day. Playing a critical role in defence, he ensured Tom Papley and other Sydney forwards never had an easy time of things at any stage, while also picking critical moments to head forward to help set up Geelong attacks. He finished with 15 disposals, four marks and five intercepts.

FULL STRETCH: Swans Tom Papley and Isaac Heeney are ready to pounce on any crumbs but are left empty-handed as Sam De Koning outreaches Sam Reid to grab one of the seven marks he took in the Grand Final. As he was all year, De Koning was a towering presence in the Geelong backline, as one of the powerful back six that held the Lions to just seven goals in the preliminary final. Such is his authority it is sometimes easy to forget that De Koning is in just his second AFL season. The 21-year-old from the Mornington Peninsula played only one match in his debut year and the Grand Final was only the 24th of his career. He would receive votes in the Norm Smith Medal and coaches' votes for his performance, made even more memorable by his first goal in AFL footy.

OUTFOXED: Forward Jeremy Cameron, here edging out Robbie Fox in a tight contest, diligently played his role for the team in his second AFL Grand Final. Cameron and his fellow big forward Tom Hawkins tag-teamed their way through 2022, with one providing support while the other starred, or vice versa. Cameron was full of praise for Hawkins after the game naming him as his mentor. "How does someone at 34 want to get better and play the way he's done? I've never had someone with so much experience right beside me when the heat of the battle's on and to bounce things off him is what it's all about." Although Hawkins claimed the headline role in the Grand Final (kicking three goals including the first two of the match), Cameron's role in the win was no less important. His aerobic capacity allowed him to cover plenty of ground on the wide expanses of the MCG, and he finished with 18 disposals. He also kicked two goals to help ensure his second Grand Final experience was much better than his first, a thrashing at the hands of Richmond in 2019 when with the GWS GIANTS. Speaking on 3AW after the win, the laidback Cameron said he was looking forward to heading back to his newly built man cave on his farm outside of Geelong, where he would enjoy "a few beers" from the keg Geelong legend and publican Billy Brownless had arranged to have delivered, and his share of hot chips slathered with barbecue sauce from his favourite local takeaway shop.

A SHOT AT GLORY: Gary Rohan looks to put Geelong further ahead as he kicks for goal in the second term. Rohan's Grand Final possession count was only seven, but his work rate was high, as he was often seen on the other side of the centre line during the afternoon, making sure Sydney's avenues to goal were never straightforward. Rohan played in Sydney's losing Grand Final teams of 2014 and 2016, so he might have had a brief pang of sympathy for his old side at game's end, but he certainly celebrated his first Premiership long and hard with his Geelong teammates.

DON'T LET GO: Late in the third quarter, with the MCG almost in full shade, the Cats were a long way ahead of the Swans and all but officially declared the 2022 Premiers. That didn't stop Tom Stewart remaining as focused as he was at the opening bounce. Stewart, a four-time All-Australian, capped off another outstanding season with a staunch defensive performance against the Swans' much-vaunted attack (16 disposals, five marks and eight intercept possessions). The Grand Final was Stewart's 126th game in the hoops, and his 87th victory. The 29-year-old is one of the game's best defenders and it's hard to fathom that he was playing local footy in the Geelong area in his early 20s before getting his chance at League level. After the game he told the *Herald Sun*, "I owe them [Geelong] everything. It's bloody brilliant. This is probably the best day of my life outside of my wedding [to Emma] and the birth of my kids [Arthur and Charlie]."

PORTLAOISE POISE: Zach Tuohy has all the poise of someone who grew up holding a Sherrin so one could be forgiven for forgetting the first 20 years of his life were spent in Ireland, where he played Gaelic football in his hometown of Portlaoise. Tuohy did what he has been doing for more than a decade on Grand Final day (his 250th AFL game), continually repelling Sydney attacks and launching Geelong forward on the way to collecting 21 disposals and taking six marks. The 32-year-old, playing in his second AFL Grand Final, also recorded seven rebound 50s, the most of any other player on the field. After the game he told AAP: "The early homesickness and the tough days ... it's kind of all been worthwhile." Referring to Geelong's misses in finals, he added: "You open yourself to criticism when you consistently just go for it and don't bottom out. To give the club this, it takes balls to do what they've done, and they deserve it. Coming to Geelong I've clearly played my best footy, but you'll have to take my word for it, I'm a much better person now as well. I'm so grateful that I was allowed to come to this club and I'll always be a Geelong person."

WITHIN REACH: Minutes away from the final siren, ruckman Rhys Stanley remains focused on the task at hand. Stanley was an emergency for the Saints' Grand Final replay loss in 2010 and on the wrong side of the equation as part of the Geelong side that went down to Richmond in the 2020 Grand Final. In an odd twist, though, Stanley had experienced a Grand Final day victory on the MCG before 2022—he won the half-time sprint as an 18-year-old in 2009. Tom Hawkins became a Premiership player for the first time that day and 13 years on, Stanley has done the same, with Hawkins as his teammate. Stanley had a game-high 27 hit-outs, setting up a torrent of centre clearances for the Cats.

COTTON:ON
COTTON:ON

COTTON:ON
AFL
Ford
SHERRIN
AFL
COTTON:ON

TOUGH SHOT: Gryan Miers gave photographers—professional and amateur—on both sides of the fence a chance at a close-up shot as he lined up for goal from outside the boundary line in the last quarter. The 23-year-old Miers, a local lad from Grovedale, was a heart-and-soul player for the Cats throughout 2022, playing 22 games and booting 13 goals. In the lead-up to the Grand Final, he told *The Age* he had developed his unique curved kicking style as a junior after watching Lance Franklin. Miers was one of many solid contributors on Grand Final day, registering 18 disposals, six marks and five score involvements.

ANTICIPATION: Is that a hint of a smile breaking out across Chris Scott's face as he addresses his troops at three-quarter time? With the Cats holding an unassailable 74-point lead with only a quarter of the game to go, who wouldn't be smiling? That smile might also have been in response to his captain's reminder to his teammates to not get carried away with their lead, and to play out the match just as they have throughout the season. Classic Selwood: give'em nothing! Scott, a two-time Premiership player with the Brisbane Lions, is now a dual Premiership coach, 11 years after becoming one in his first season at the helm. Two days after the emphatic win, Scott told Fox Footy's *AFL 360* program he was prepared to leave the club at the end of last season after his team was smacked by Melbourne in the preliminary final. Scott asked a select group of players if he still had their support. "I said, 'if you have any doubt at all you have to tell me.' I have done a version of that [meeting] almost every year, but at the end of '21 in particular they were emphatic, and the support was the basis of my drive in 2022."

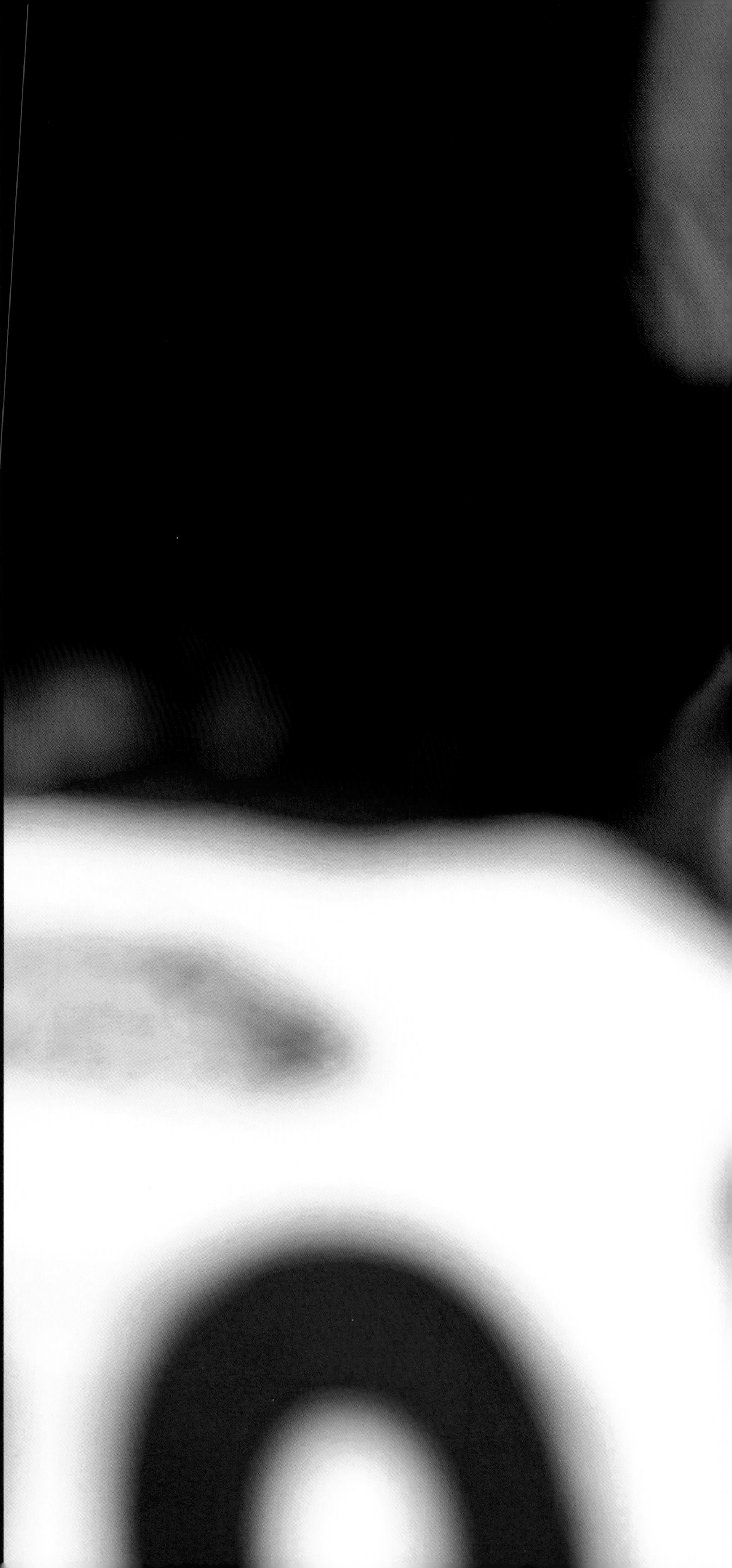

Ford
GMHBa

MOBBED: What better time to kick your first AFL goal than in the last quarter of a Grand Final! That's what Sam De Koning did, and his teammates, Brad Close (left), Gryan Miers (32) and Mark Blicavs (right) are at least as happy as he is about it. Perhaps not so was Patrick Dangerfield whose snapshot would have gone through had not De Koning made that late snatch on the line. Sydney's Jake Lloyd can do no more than look on forlornly. De Koning is not alone in scoring his first AFL goal in a Grand Final. Among others, Richmond's Marlion Pickett did it on debut in 2019 in the Tigers' victory over the GWS GIANTS and Brisbane's Richard Hadley kicked his first goal in the Lions' 2003 Grand Final against Collingwood.

FIFTEEN MINUTES OF FAME: According to the website *ancestry.com*, the surname 'Parfitt' derives from the Middle English word 'parfit', meaning 'fully trained, well versed'. That's exactly what Brandan Parfitt was in his role as the Cats' medical substitute, having been told of his inclusion in the 23 on Friday. Within a minute of coming on to replace the injured Cam Guthrie in the last quarter, Parfitt had scored a goal and was celebrating with teammate Jeremy Cameron. Parfitt certainly made the most of his time on the field, which came in at 15 minutes, collecting eight touches. He told the *Herald Sun* of his elevation to the starting 23 when Max Holmes was ruled out with his hamstring strain: "I always knew I was in the mix, but you don't really know. I found out last night [Friday], so it was pretty crazy. I am pretty devastated for Holmesy. I love him as a good mate, but that's footy." He added he was looking to make an impact when he took the field. "I was so keen to get the footy in my hands. I didn't want to be out there with no touches." And that goal? "'Closey' handballed it over his head and I was in the goalsquare and kicked it and then I celebrated like a goose!"

ICING ON THE CAKE: With his team ahead by 75 points and a Premiership within reach, Cats skipper Joel Selwood was still working as hard at the 24-minute mark of the final term as he was in the game's opening 60 seconds. Accepting a deft tap from teammate Brad Close, Selwood threw the ball onto the outside of his boot from just inside the 50-metre mark as Swan Dylan Stephens crashed into him. The ball sailed through, Selwood's goal capping off a magnificent 27-possession captain's game. When he announced his retirement four days later he said of that goal: "It was probably the best goal I have ever kicked."

STACKS ON!: The moment after Joel Selwood kicked that outside-of-the-boot last-quarter goal, his old mate Patrick Dangerfield lifted him from the turf by his jumper, and he was immediately mobbed by a swarm of other teammates, including Gary Rohan (23), Tom Hawkins (back, facing camera), Jake Kolodjashnij (8), Rhys Stanley (1) and Isaac Smith, who still had enough energy to leap over the entire horde of Cats. No surprises there: the AFL's picture files are full of Smith embracing teammates—it's part of his DNA! The embrace that followed lasted more than a few seconds, a measure of how much Selwood has meant to his comrades. To many watching on, it was a sign some in the team might also have been saying an on-field goodbye to their leader. Said Hawkins after the game when asked what he told his skipper and mate: "I told him he is a Premiership captain. It's such a wonderful sport, but you rarely get opportunities like that. We have achieved some wonderful things, but to be able to do this after the year he's had and just our time in the game—it's just so special."

Ford
8
AFL
Ford
AFL
COTTON:ON

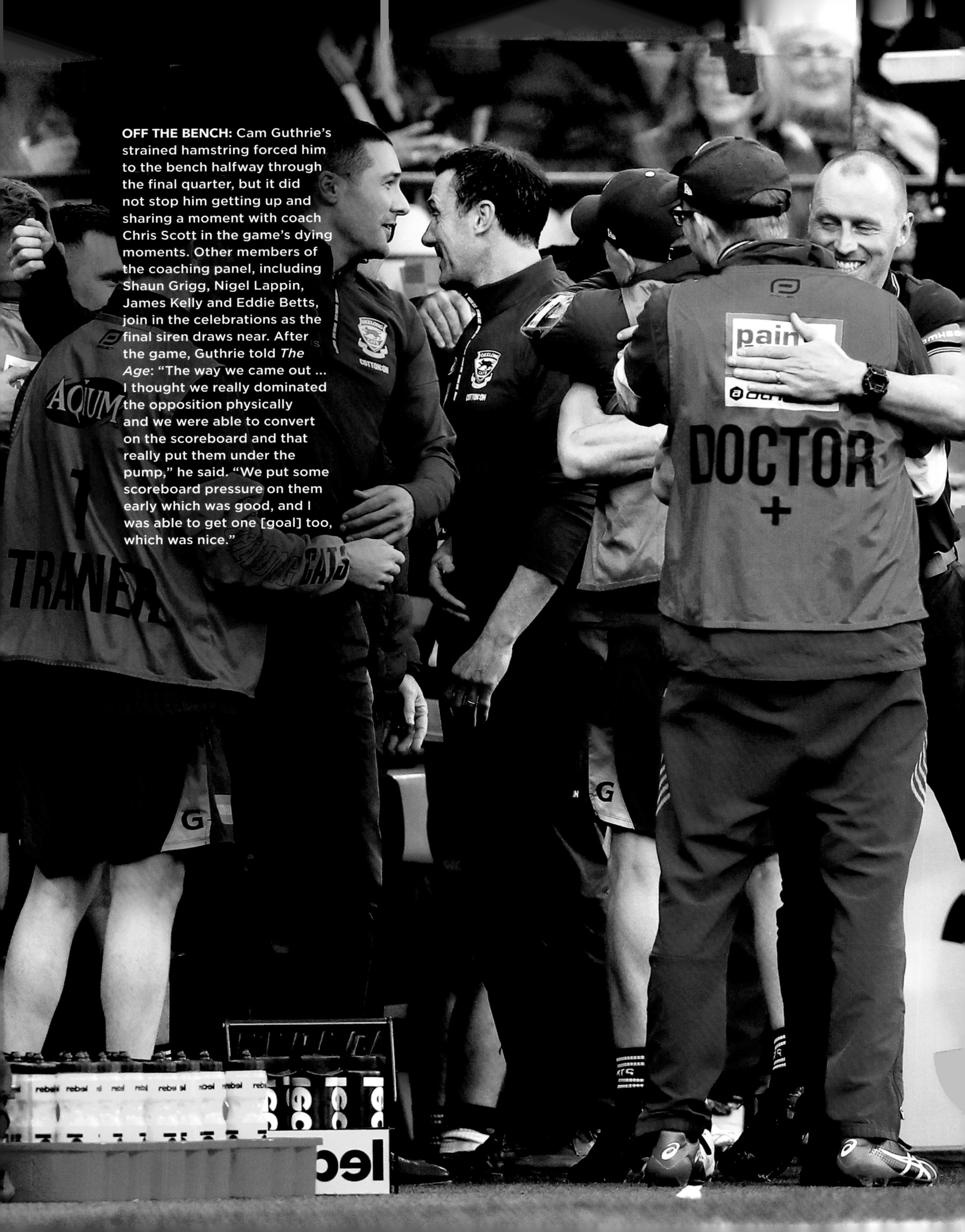

OFF THE BENCH: Cam Guthrie's strained hamstring forced him to the bench halfway through the final quarter, but it did not stop him getting up and sharing a moment with coach Chris Scott in the game's dying moments. Other members of the coaching panel, including Shaun Grigg, Nigel Lappin, James Kelly and Eddie Betts, join in the celebrations as the final siren draws near. After the game, Guthrie told *The Age*: "The way we came out ... I thought we really dominated the opposition physically and we were able to convert on the scoreboard and that really put them under the pump," he said. "We put some scoreboard pressure on them early which was good, and I was able to get one [goal] too, which was nice."

29
Ford
AFL

FOR THE FAITHFUL

Geelong's 2022 Premiership was about many things, including faith, perseverance, trust and, after 11 years of 'if only' results, redemption. It was about toiling in the face of perceived failure, believing the desired result would eventually come. It was about honesty and unity. It was about making harsh but realistic decisions aimed at protecting the team and the club. Above all, it was about nurturing people.

The Cats' fourth Premiership of the 21st century (equal with Hawthorn's record) confirmed them as the most successful team of this millennium, with 349 wins from 522 games since the start of 2001—41 more victories than the next best club, the Sydney Swans.

But as coach Chris Scott has learned in his 12 seasons in charge, only the ultimate prize counts. He is now a dual Premiership coach after his direction had kept Geelong mostly near the top of the tree without anything substantial to show for it. In the face of criticism from some, Scott remained resolute about the club's team-building methods coupled with his insistence on resting stars and being ultra-cautious when managing those returning from injury. If critics claimed his win in 2011, his first season in charge, was with a team that others had built, then they had to acknowledge the 2022 victory had his fingerprints all over it. Not that he would ever make that point, for Scott's way has been about constantly reassessing his methods and systems, taking counsel, exploring alternative ways, making tough but necessary decisions and communicating them consistently and appropriately, always with the good of the team in mind.

"It does feel like it's been a really long, challenging road," Scott said after the Grand Final victory. "We've been consistent. It feels like it's been a bit of a cruel game because we've done everything we could to give all our people a chance and with that comes great emotional risk if you don't get it done at the end of the season. Hopefully, even for those people who struggled with us over the journey, this is for them too," he said.

Before addressing the media, in those ultra-sweet moments immediately after the final siren, Scott and his lieutenants savoured the victory with players—including those who were not part of the winning 23—officials, families and fans—Geelong people all. It was a brilliant scene full of tears and hugs and shouting and fist pumps, something we see after every Grand Final, but something we never tire of, for everyone embroiled amid these scenes has their unique story.

Significant among those tales was that of Patrick Dangerfield, the superstar who had logged 302 games without a Premiership. He now had one, finally, after agreeing to play the patient game with his constant injuries "This is Everest," he told Channel 7. "This is what it means to be content. It's worth the wait and better than I could have imagined. It's bloody special."

Then there was the veteran Isaac Smith, having played one of the games of his life to win the Norm Smith Medal, just days after the death of his beloved grandpa Kevin. Smith was a humble but worthy winner. "I feel a little bit embarrassed ... but it is something I'm very proud to wear," he said..

There was Brandan Parfitt, who had come on as the medical sub for a quick but brilliant cameo. Near him was Max Holmes, a revelation in 2022, but a mere onlooker on the biggest day of the season, ruled out because of injury. Sliding doors and all that.

There were the Guthrie brothers, Cam and Zach, making a salt-of-the-earth football family as proud as punch. Father Andrew, using his step-dad's surname, Merryweather, played six games for Fitzroy and Essendon in 1980s; grandfather Byron played four games for Footscray in the 1950s.

There was Tyson Stengle, previously discarded by two other AFL clubs, now an AFL Premiership winner. There were the Irishmen, Zach Tuohy and Mark O'Connor, not just blue and white heroes, but heroes to their families and friends back home.

And there was skipper Joel Selwood, who, with Scott, had finally hoisted the Premiership Cup, a moment that had taken more than 4000 days.

"This is for everyone," he said in the rooms afterwards, reprising a similar sentiment to that Scott had put out on the podium earlier. "To everyone who has worked so hard to get us to this position, I hope they're sitting back proud." **G**

Peter Di Sisto

TAKING IT ALL IN: Joel Selwood has experienced it before—three times, in fact—but that does not take away from the enormity of winning another AFL Premiership. One difference between Selwood's first three flags and this one is that his 2022 win has come as captain. He wasn't just *part* of a Premiership team he had *led* his side to Premiership glory. Off the field, Selwood's life has also undergone significant change. A couple of weeks before the flag win, he and wife Brit announced they were expecting their first child after years of fertility struggles. Little wonder the Geelong warrior put his hands to his face in a quiet moment after the match to reflect on footy and family milestones. Said Selwood later: "The day got to me a little bit. We've just been building for it for so long." And, as we would learn just days later, further change for the skipper was coming.

UNITED IN TRIUMPH: The siren has sounded and the reality hits for Tom Stewart, Patrick Dangerfield, Rhys Stanley, Jake Kolodjashnij and Brandan Parfitt: they are now Premiership players. The slumped form of a vanquished Swan, Tom Hickey, in the background makes for a stark contrast to the jubilation of this quintet of Cats. The five arrived at this moment via diverse pathways. Stewart and Dangerfield both grew up in the Geelong region, but the latter's first eight AFL seasons were spent in Adelaide with the Crows, while Stewart played locally for South Barwon, having missed selection in several national drafts. The other three were born outside Victoria: Stanley in Berri in South Australia, coming to Geelong via St Kilda; Kolodjashnij is a Tasmanian from Launceston and Parfitt was born in Darwin and played his junior footy there for Nightcliff.

35
Ford
AFL
COTTON:ON

Ford
GEELONG
CATS
FOOTBALL CLUB
AFL

▲ **TRIBUTE:** To take the stage and address the crowd after being comprehensively thrashed in a Grand Final would be an unenviable challenge, but Sydney's co-captain Dane Rampe delivered his post-match speech with integrity, humility and due deference to the victors. That Rampe singled out his Geelong counterpart for a special mention is a measure of the respect those outside Geelong hold for the Cats skipper. "I just want to touch on Joel Selwood's record," said Rampe, looking towards the Premiership skipper. "Sometimes you have to pinch yourself when you share the field with giants of the game, mate, and you're an absolute giant. Congratulations." In the background is the day's MC, Hamish McLachlan.

◀ **EMOTIONAL EMBRACE:** Joel Selwood and Tom Hawkins made their AFL debuts for Geelong in 2007 and their careers have run more or less in parallel. In fact, their shared journey began even earlier than the year of their first game together. When drafted in 2006, the pair found themselves living together with the same host family. They had taken different pathways to the club but quickly formed a strong bond. "We came from different backgrounds," said Selwood. "Mine was with the family in Bendigo and 'Hawk' was on the farm and in the boarding house. It was nice to have each other to lean on." The closeness of the pair, and the emotion that came with the win after coming so close so many times since their 2011 success is clear, as Hawkins is drawn to tears in the embrace. Having played their first game together (round two in 2007), the 2022 Grand Final was the 305th game featuring Selwood and Hawkins together on the field (217 of those were wins). Hawkins was not part of Selwood's first Premiership in 2007, but they have now played together in three winning Grand Finals, 2009, 2011 and 2022.

SILVERWARE FOR A SILVER FOX: Tom Atkins, Jed Bews, Brandan Parfitt, Jeremy Cameron (obscured) and Zach Tuohy are all smiles as they congratulate Isaac Smith on being named the winner of the Norm Smith Medal. There's a hint of grey in 33-year-old Isaac Smith's hair, but his advancing years have not slowed him down. "A few people were writing us silver foxes off, but there's still a little bit in the tank," Smith told Channel 7. Accepting the medal, Smith paid tribute to his late grandfather Kevin, who died on the Wednesday before the Grand Final. Asked later if his 'Pop' had inspired his best-on-ground performance, Smith responded, "I don't know. I don't win awards like this often, or ever, so maybe he did." Smith collected a game-high 32 possessions, had 14 score involvements and kicked three goals, two in a dynamic first-quarter burst.

TOYOTA
TOYOTA
TOYOTA
Ford
GEELONG CATS
AFL
COTTON:ON
AFL
COTTON:ON
AFL
COTTON:ON
GMHBA

CROWNING ACHIEVEMENT: It's the moment every captain and coach dreams of. Standing on the dais with a Premiership medal (captain) and Jock McHale Medal (coach) around the neck, arms aloft, each with one hand on the Premiership Cup. Chris Scott has now done it twice, his second flag as coach coming 11 years after his first, that a rare achievement, winning a flag in his first season at the wheel. For Selwood, this was his first as leader having taken the baton from Cameron Ling in 2012. Each leader has won four Premierships as player or

coach. In his post-match press conference, Scott lamented not having made mention, while on stage, of the players who did not play in the Grand Final. Citing Max Holmes and Sam Menegola among others, he said: "We should spare a moment for those who have worked so hard to get us to this point and may well be feeling that they haven't been as integral as the guys that got to take the field. Nothing could be further from the truth."

PREMIERS IN PROFILE: The 'storming of the stage' by the winning players following the presentation of the Premiership Cup is now a well-established tradition, as is the follow-up winning team's photo. In the ensuing days, weeks, months and years, the front-on shot of that celebration will adorn newspapers, magazines, the cover of this book, and walls in sheds, offices and other workplaces—as a reminder of that moment of triumph. AFL Photos photographer Cameron Spencer took a slightly different approach to the moment, opting for a side-on shot, saving for posterity an alternative view of that memorable moment. Coach and captain Chris Scott and Joel Selwood (holding the cup) have experienced this euphoria before but, other than Mitch Duncan, Tom Hawkins and Isaac Smith, this was a first.

AFL
COTTON:ON

NORM SMITH
MEDAL
COTTON:ON
AFL
GRAND FINAL
2022
Ford
GEELONG
CATS
FOOTBALL CLUB

▲ **REDEMPTION:** When Geelong was considering taking Tyson Stengle on board as a delisted free agent in late 2021, new assistant/development coach Eddie Betts voiced his approval and offered to mentor the ex-Tiger and Crow if he was recruited. Stengle had encountered some off-field struggles in his previous years as an AFL player, but Betts thought the Cats would be the right fit for him. The pair had met at Adelaide in 2019. "I played one game with Eddie at the Crows," said Stengle. "That was a pretty cool moment. I idolised him as a younger kid." A cool moment, indeed. The pair kicked nine goals between them in that game, Stengle snaring three of them. With Betts as a mentor, Stengle has shone, playing every game in 2022 to become the first delisted player to be an All-Australian and first to win a flag. He played no small part in the win, kicking four goals to be part of a Premiership, something that eluded Betts as a player, having played in Adelaide's 2017 loss to Richmond. Stengle acknowledged that he couldn't have done it without his idol, friend and confidant. "It means a lot. He helped me throughout my hard times, and I've got good times here now. He was crying after the game. It shows how proud he is of me. I'm just proud that I've given back to him."

◀ **OLD STAGERS:** In a statistical quirk, in the two Grand Finals that have been decided by 81 points, the winner of the Norm Smith Medal has been a 33-year-old. In 1980 it was Richmond's Kevin Bartlett, in 2022 Isaac Smith claimed the prize. At 33 years and 268 days, Smith was 63 days older than Bartlett was on his big day, but Bartlett's premature hair loss and light frame made him look rather older. Smith has tinges of grey running through his wavy locks, but his best-on-ground performance suggests he still has plenty more to offer the Cats. His Premiership medal joins the three already in his trophy cabinet, from his days as a significant force in Hawthorn's three-peat (2013-2015). Smith and Bartlett are the two oldest Norm Smith medallists, ahead of Carlton's Greg Williams, who won the medal in 1995 on his 32nd birthday.

KING OF THE KIDS: Joel Selwood's on-field credentials as a player and captain have never been in doubt, but in the latter stages of his career the wider community has become aware of his off-field efforts. Those efforts received recognition on Brownlow Medal night, when he was presented with the 2022 Jim Stynes Award for his years of service to the community. In more than 1000 hours with Geelong's Cats Community program, Selwood has been a regular at school and club visits, AFL Auskick clinics, community camps and country days and has promoted inclusive footy by launching the AFL Barwon Region Access All-Abilities Auskick clinics in 2021. Selwood exemplified that dedication to the community and kids when he posed for a photo with the young Auskickers dressed in Cats gear who presented the Premiership medallions to the players. Earlier, when receiving his medal, he handed over his Grand Final boots to the Auskicker of the year, Archie Stockdale, from Natimuk in western Victoria.

TOYOTA
Ford
AFL
GEELONG
CATS
nab
Auskick

PADDY WHACK: Coach Chris Scott gives Patrick Dangerfield a pat on the tummy as they share a moment after the final siren. In the lead-up to the game, Scott said the management of players this season had been a significant focus, citing Dangerfield's condition as evidence of that. "He's in really good shape," Scott said. "Compared to where he's been previously, it's chalk and cheese. He's a bit older but he goes into the biggest game of the year in the best shape he's been in for four years." Scott's assessment was borne out on the day with Dangerfield finishing runner-up in the Norm Smith Medal voting. Several pundits thought he was unlucky not to win the medal. Dangerfield was later named winner of the Gary Ayres Medal as the best player of the finals, as voted by the coaches involved.

COTTON:ON
Ford
GEELONG
CATS

SIBLINGS SHINE: The emergence of Cam Guthrie (right) in recent seasons as one of the most consistent midfielders in the AFL has been critical to Geelong's push for another Premiership. The 30-year-old ball magnet loves the hard stuff and provides the perfect back-up for veteran midfielders and similar hard nuts Joel Selwood, Patrick Dangerfield and Mitch Duncan. Along the way, his support of younger brother Zach (left) has been pivotal in helping the 24-year-old, medium-sized defender gain confidence that he, too, belongs at AFL level. Zach said of Cam's support: "He has been really influential in helping me get to this point," admitting he might never have realised his Premiership ambitions without his big brother there to guide him. "I don't think so," Zach told the *Herald Sun* after the Grand Final. "He has been massive for me. Just having him in my corner has been huge." On Grand Final day, the Guthrie boys became just the fifth set of brothers to win Premierships at Geelong and they are only the fourth pairing in club history to achieve the feat in the same team. The others in Geelong's illustrious group are Gary Jnr (2007 and 2009) and Nathan Ablett (2007), the twins, Alistair and Stewart Lord (1963), Les and Peter Hardiman (1931 and 1937), and Len (1931) and Jack Metherell (1937). Against Sydney, Cam Guthrie had 16 disposals, five tackles and a goal, while Zach had 15 disposals on a day the Guthrie family will never forget. Cam said of his brother: "I'm so proud of Zach and how hard he has worked to get to where he is now. He deserved to be here today with a medal around his neck."

coles
AFL PREMIERS 2022
AFL
GRAND FINAL
2022
GEELONG
CATS
FOOTBALL CLUB

PARTY TIME: After a season to cherish, Geelong's 21-year-old defender Sam De Koning was ready to get the party started as soon as the final siren sounded. The Cats had the game sewn up early, allowing players to soak up the atmosphere and enjoy the moment, a rare thing in any match. For De Koning, who finished runner-up to Collingwood's Nick Daicos in the 2022 NAB AFL Rising Star award and, along the way, showed he was one of the best up-and-coming intercept defenders in the competition, it was time to let loose and celebrate. Post-game, his skipper Joel Selwood offered some sound words of advice. De Koning told the *Herald Sun*: "The siren goes and I was a bit loose. I thought all the boys were going to go as hard as I did, but it turns out I was the only one." Selwood, always the wise head, told his younger teammates to "be responsible" and "remember the moment". De Koning certainly had reason to be proud of his performance in what was just his 24th game. On top of 16 disposals, his intercept marking in the opening quarter was pivotal in halting Sydney's avenues to goal. In the last quarter, De Koning got to cap off his day when he drifted forward late in the game to mark Patrick Dangerfield's shot at goal and slam the ball through from point blank range. Quite the stage for one's first goal in League football! The coaches were impressed with his game, awarding him 1.5 votes in the coaches' award, seemingly sharing a three-pointer with Mark Blicavs.

Ford
GEELONG
CATS
EST
1859
FOOTBALL CLUB
AFL PREMIERS 2022

SMILING SAMMY: A regular at Geelong training and on the sidelines in recent seasons has been their 'water boy' and unofficial club mascot Sam Moorfoot, a 29-year-old Cats fanatic with Down syndrome who, with his infectious smile, has become a much-loved member of the club's inner sanctum. He was offered a job at Kardinia Park after his parents helped him write a letter to then-CEO Brian Cook in 2014, asking for work at the club, and ever since, at the Cats' main training session each week, Moorfoot delivers water to the players and helps behind the scenes. Captain Joel Selwood said of Moorfoot's impact on the club: "He's just good for the boys, good for our morale. Sam brings a happy face in every time. He works hard in the morning, has lunch with us and then, apparently, does absolutely nothing when he gets home! He's an extremely positive person, Sammy." As the jubilant Geelong players walked their victory lap after beating Sydney, Selwood spotted Moorfoot in the crowd and invited him to join the players on the arena. The look on Moorfoot's face was one of the standout images of the post-game celebrations. That joy turned to pure elation when goalkicker Jeremy Cameron (pictured smiling behind Moorfoot, with Sam De Koning to his right) draped his Premiership medallion over Moorfoot's neck. Moorfoot returned the favour two days later, dressing as the key forward at the club's traditional 'Mad Monday' post-season get-together.

coles
2022
Ford
GEELONG
CATS
FOOTBALL CLUB
2022

KEY CATS: Jed Bews and Mark Blicavs (here posing with the Premiership Cup before adoring supporters) had vastly different roles on Grand Final day, but both proved crucial in helping Geelong secure its 10th VFL/AFL Premiership. Bews—whose father, Andrew, played 207 games for the Cats (from 1982-93) and was one of the best afield in the team's six-point Grand Final loss to Hawthorn in 1989—was given the job of negating Sydney's energetic dangerman Tom Papley, a role he performed admirably. Papley, who kicked three goals in Sydney's one-point preliminary final victory over Collingwood, gathered 20 disposals in the Grand Final, but was always under pressure and managed just a solitary late goal. Blicavs was one of Geelong's best performers, earning a Norm Smith Medal vote from dual winner and voting chairman Andrew McLeod for his non-stop running, tap work and willingness to support teammates all over the field—add to that 1.5 votes from the coaches. Blicavs' first-quarter goal, the Cats' third, struck an early body blow to Sydney's psyche. After the game, Bews spoke of his parents' influence on his career, telling the *Herald Sun*: "Both Mum (Julie-Ann) and Dad are a huge support for me. They have been massive for helping me live out my dreams." Knowing Andrew came so close in 1989, Jed said the 2022 triumph was "as much for him as for me."

MELBOURNE CRICKET CLUB
2022MEMBER
ATS
GEELONG
AFL

REPAYING THE FAITH: As he basked in the afterglow of Premiership victory, defender and vice-captain Tom Stewart (pictured with the Premiership Cup among jubilant supporters) was grateful for the faith invested in him by everyone at Geelong. Recruited from AFL Barwon Football Netball League club, South Barwon, in 2016 at the mature age of 22, Stewart's first VFL-level game for the club was almost his last as doubts crept in about whether he was capable of making the leap to the AFL. Stewart told *afl.com.au* earlier this year: "We played out here [at GMHBA Stadium] and I think it was a Thursday night game against the Northern Blues. Shane O'Bree, our VFL coach, let me know during the week that I was playing on Liam Jones. He gave me a bath, kicked five on me, and he went back into the ones [for Carlton] and never went back to the VFL. It was a bit of a sliding doors moment. I was always of the opinion that if it didn't work out, I would go back to South [Barwon] fitter, more professional and a better player. I got named again the following week and I think I had 24 or 25 [disposals] and kicked two [goals] off a back flank and that set me up for the rest of the year." Stewart has become one of—if not the finest—intercept defender in the game, equally adept at shutting down opponents while also turning defence into attack. Coach Chris Scott spoke glowingly of his defender, as a player and a man. "I've known Tom for a long time, and he is a ... a fantastic, strong character—fundamental to what we do at Geelong. When my time's come, I'll look back and say I was honoured to have known and coached Tom Stewart."

TIMELY CAMEO: If Brandan Parfitt—a late inclusion in the reshuffled side as the medical substitute after Max Holmes was forced to withdraw through injury—had had a dream on the night before the Grand Final, it might have gone something like this. Geelong would get off to a flying start and, when the game was effectively won, a teammate would suffer a minor injury, paving the way for him to see some Grand Final action, maybe even sneak a goal, enough for a great yarn to tell the grandkids later in life. Well, that's exactly how it played out. Halfway through the final quarter, with Geelong having sewn up its 10th League Premiership, Cam Guthrie limped from the field with hamstring tightness and was immediately subbed out of the game. Parfitt took his place and drifted forward where, just like in his dream, he snapped a clever goal and was mobbed by teammates. The Cats could do no wrong, and now all 23 players who made the final cut had contributed to the stunning 81-point victory. Parfitt's eight disposals in barely 15 minutes of game time was more than six Sydney players obtained for the day, such was his desperation to leave his imprint on a Geelong Premiership. It's no wonder he was beaming from ear to ear when the chance came to hold the Premiership Cup aloft. Having arrived at Geelong from the Northern Territory via the 2016 NAB AFL Draft (pick 26), the 24-year-old small forward now has 112 games under his belt, and has played in two Grand Finals (he experienced the loss to Richmond in 2020).

TIME FOR MATES: After two years without an AFL final in Victoria due to the pandemic, the MCG was open to everybody in 2022 as crowds flocked back in their droves to witness a thrilling finals series. Three finals were decided by six points or less, with six under four goals. Geelong were the only team to produce blow-outs in September, defeating the Brisbane Lions by 71 points in the preliminary final, then the Sydney Swans by 81 in the Grand Final. No wonder defender Jack Henry (pictured second from left) wanted his mates to join him on the field for the Premiership celebrations. Henry had held superstar Lance 'Buddy' Franklin goalless for the first time in a Grand Final.

AUSTRALIA
FOOTBALL LEA
2022
PREMIERSHIP
WON BY
Kathmandu

TOYOTA
AFL PREMIERS 2022

'BROTHERS': In a 2022 season full of remarkable twists and turns, the fairytale comeback of Tyson Stengle, (right) and the late inclusion of Brandan Parfitt as medical sub in the Grand Final, must surely rank among the best of them. Stengle, recruited as a free agent, proved the standout small forward of the competition, playing all 25 games and kicking 53 goals, including a game-high four in the Grand Final. Fellow Indigenous star Parfitt was a lucky last-minute inclusion in the 23, told on the eve of the final he would be included, after Max Holmes was ruled out with the hamstring strain suffered late in the preliminary final.

FAMILY CLUB: The backbone of Geelong's remarkable recent era of dominance (four Premierships from six Grand Finals starting in 2007) is its deliberately cultivated and celebrated family-first culture. One in, all in. Young men such as (CLOCKWISE FROM TOP LEFT) Patrick Dangerfield (pictured with wife Mardi and daughter Felicity), Rhys Stanley (with wife Kirsten, daughter Sloane and son Jagger), Tom Hawkins (with partner Emma Clapham and their daughters, Arabella and Primrose) and Mitch Duncan (with partner Demi Miles and their three children, Ollie, Scarlett and Archie) and Isaac Smith (with wife Candice and daughter Isla), share the journey together on the field, then spend time together with partners and children off the field, riding the highs of success and the disappointments of injury or defeat, always conscious of embracing and supporting one another along the way. Those shared journeys make moments such as these scenes post-game on Grand Final day all the more special for everyone involved.

GATHER 'ROUND THE CUP: The club's theme song was sung after all but four games throughout the dominant 2022 season, but it was the on-ground singalong on Grand Final day that everyone had been waiting for. With the Premiership Cup taking prominence, players and staff belted out a boisterous rendition ofWe Are Geelong for the first time as a club on Grand Final day since the 2011 victory over Collingwood. The first person coach Chris Scott hugged in the rooms after singing the song was legendary recruiter Stephen Wells, who has continued presenting the winning coach with playing lists that have given the club the best chance to deliver ongoing success. Scott's 71.3 per cent winning record as a coach (204 wins and two draws in 286 games) is the best win-loss percentage of any coach in League history in charge in at least 80 games. After Scott finally released him from his bear hug, Wells told the *Herald Sun*: "I'm feeling very excited, very proud, so relieved, and so happy for Chris and everyone involved." Club CEO Steve Hocking, also in the *Herald Sun*, praised Scott's ability to empower his players, believing it to be a key to his evolution, longevity, and success. "It's a pretty bold thing to do, because there are so many young players. A lot of coaches would look at it and go, 'Why are you empowering them that far and what if they make a mistake?' But Chris's view is that it's not about the mistake, it's about the learning that comes from it. He's been exceptional in terms of allowing that ability for the players to be expansive in the way they play and their decision-making. It's a real credit to him that he's created that environment."

AFL
GRAND FINAL
2022
Ford
TOYOTA
coles
Recycal
United

MEMORABLE MILESTONE: With a Portlaoise flag draped over his shoulders as a tribute to his Irish hometown, and his former GAA club, County Laois, Zach Tuohy has been a great example that the best of Ireland's Gaelic game can make it at the highest level of Australian football. Tuohy can certainly scrap and fight with the best the AFL has to offer, but he can also slice the opposition to ribbons with his precise skills by hand and foot, outsmart you with his astute reading of the game, and settle the most intense of situations with his coolness and composure under pressure. A consistent big-game performer, Tuohy quickly found his place in defence and through the midfield under Chris Scott, having previously played 120 games for Carlton (from 2011-16). In 2020, he joined the late Melbourne champion Jim Stynes (264 games from 1987-98) as the only two players born in Ireland to play 200 VFL/AFL games. In a quirk of fate, Tuohy's 250th happened to fall on Grand Final day, in a milestone match he and his family and friends watching back home will never forget. After being chaired from the field, cup in hand, by Rhys Stanley and countryman Mark O'Connor (obscured), and cheered on by teammates including Patrick Dangerfield, far left, Gary Rohan, Jake Kolodjashnij, Jed Bews, Mark Blicavs and Sam De Koning, Tuohy said after the game: "I'm not done yet, but it feels a bit full circle, like this is kind of what it all led to. The early homesickness and the tough days, it's all been worthwhile. Coming to Geelong, I've clearly played my best footy, but, and you'll have to take my word for it, I'm a much better person now as well. The club has good values and treats its people really well. I'm just so grateful I was allowed to come to this club and I'll always be a Geelong person."

THE GEELONG WAY

Such was the Cats' early dominance that their fans, at the MCG, those at home and in pubs and other venues around the country, were rightly relaxed and able to enjoy the demolition. This was an exhibition to savour, with none of the edge-of-seat anxiety that comes when big games are too tight to call.

Not surprisingly, before the result was official, supporters were milling around Moorabool and Ryrie Streets, in the heart of Geelong, their numbers (and hearts) swelling as soon as the final siren sounded. The emissions from a boom box blasting the club song, combined with car horns, air horns, the bellowing of fans shouting into megaphones, screaming kids and a smattering of barking dogs (yes, dogs joining a gathering for cats) made for a catastrophe of noise, the fans' jubilation, in part encouraged by the liquid refreshments some in the throng had earlier consumed.

"When Geelong wins—and especially winning the flag—the town is up for 12 months, the sun comes up and the days are good," supporter Craig Watson told the ABC. He was speaking for many.

It would be a long but memorable night for many, and only the start of days of celebrations that would see tens of thousands of fans (including youngsters who weren't born when the Cats last saluted in 2011) at events including a family day at Kardinia Park the day after the win, and a street parade on the following Tuesday when players travelled in cars from Upper Eastern Beach Road to Streampacket Gardens overlooking Corio Bay, where they were again lauded.

And, although nobody will ever take that flag away, reality hits hard in professional sport. On the Wednesday, a quintet of players (Quinton Narkle, Francis Evans, Nick Stevens, Paul Tsapatolis and Zane Williams) was farewelled after being delisted, just hours before the most important Cat of all, Joel Selwood, bid his own farewell. The skipper's exit might have jolted many still-celebrating fans, but it was not unexpected. If anything, it was a reminder that change is a constant at all football clubs.

And without significant change at the end of the 2021 season, Geelong people might not have had the chance to celebrate the club's 10th flag. In the wake of a terrible Preliminary Final loss to Melbourne, there was an overhaul of the coaching team and the football department more broadly. Geelong's three-time Premiership midfielder, James Kelly and Richmond's 2017 Mr Versatility, Shaun Grigg, were instrumental in offering and executing new ideas, while the team focused hard during pre-season on adapting a "go forward' mentality, moving away from the defend-first approach of seasons past while taking more risks with the ball. The introduction of high-quality young players who were ready to go helped change the dynamic of the squad, while a greater emphasis on making sure small forwards kept the ball inside 50 returned dividends. The Cats, as good as they had been over the past decade, played a more rounded game in 2022, every player knowing his role and understanding that it would take the full efforts of 23 players each week—not the outlandish acts of one or two—to deliver what they all wanted at season's end. The mathematical outcomes of these philosophical and practical changes helped tell the story: Geelong kicked an average of 18 more points per game in 2022 than 2021 (99 to 81) while staying miserly in the back half in conceding 66 points per outing (69 in 2021).

There was nothing new here, in truth. Coach Chris Scott has adapted his team's approach each season in part based on the personnel available to him. Less than a week after the Grand Final win, there were already eight holes to fill on the list (Luke Dahlhaus announced his retirement the day after Selwood's departure, while Shaun Higgins had done the same through the finals), with the bulk of the newbies to come during the trade and free agency signing period and the AFL Draft later in the year.

Some of those additions might well allow Scott the luxury of smoothing any perceived wrinkles in his game plan for 2023 (were there any?). But before we look too far ahead, it's worth recalling that the 2022 team was undefeated for more than four months on the way to the flag, and the club has been peerless over more than two decades when it comes to winning.

We know with certainty the Cats will continue to play with courage, commitment, and conviction. They know no other way. **G**

Peter Di Sisto

ONE FOR ALL AGES: This young Geelong supporter, captured watching the Cats' street party on the Tuesday after the Grand Final, wasn't alive when her team last tasted Premiership success, in 2011. But, unlike the long 44-year wait that many diehard supporters endured between the 1963 and 2007 Grand Final victories, this little girl has been fortunate to witness her Cats win the big one before she even starts school! Hours after cheering and celebrating Geelong's dominant victory over Sydney, Cats supporters of all ages flocked to the streets of Geelong to catch a glimpse of their heroes. In a relatively short span, four Premiership parties have been held in Geelong (2007, 2009, 2011 and 2022), marking one of the most dominant eras in the game's history. On the back of this most recent triumph, expect to see many more young children proudly wearing blue and white hoops in the years ahead.

KINGS OF GEELONG: When Billy Brownless (pictured with Premiership captain Joel Selwood) famously kicked his match-winning goal after the siren in the 1994 Qualifying Final against Footscray, Channel 7 commentator Sandy Roberts dubbed him "the king of Geelong". Certainly, Brownless—who played in four losing Grand Finals (1989, 1992, 1994-95) for the Cats—revels in a Geelong Premiership as much as anyone. The day after cheering his team home against Sydney, Brownless hosted the club's family day, where he declared Selwood "the Pope", summarising the lofty status the four-time Premiership champion and Geelong games-record-holder has in the city and across the game.

SHADY SCENE: After a night of revelling, victorious Geelong players arrived at the club's Sunday family day on the outskirts of Kardinia Park a little worse for wear. Nothing gives away a Premiership player's wellbeing after winning a Grand Final more than the wearing of sunglasses to shield weary eyes. And why wouldn't they party long through the night, having ended 11 years of struggle and finals heartbreak to finally secure the club's 10th VFL/AFL flag. If you add the seven they won in the VFA era—1870 to 1896—the Cats' tally of Premierships at the highest level is behind only Carlton (22) and Essendon (20). Only Patrick Dangerfield, Tom Hawkins, Zach Tuohy, Tom Atkins, Sam De Koning, Norm Smith Medal winner Isaac Smith and coach Chris Scott were 'brave' enough to expose their eyes to the elements for this special photograph.

STRALIAN
OTBALL LEAGUE
2022
EMIERSHIP CUP
Ford
GMHBA
51

SEA OF CATS: Thousands of jubilant Geelong supporters swarmed to the club's supporters' day after seeing their team dominate from siren to siren to secure a famous Premiership. The town known as 'Sleepy Hollow' was anything but snoozy on this day, as songs were sung, hugs shared, backs slapped and cheers given. For the fourth time in the last 15 years, the AFL Premiership Cup had come "home", as Joel Selwood so proudly stated after the game. The club set a new benchmark for membership numbers in 2022, and it seemed a significant number of the Cats' 71,943 members had joined with the players and staff to soak up their success.

END OF AN ERA

The signs were there on Grand Final day that the career of one of the game's all-time greats was about to come to an end. And what an end. When Joel Selwood roved a teammate's tap, steadied, and with the outside of his trusty right boot, curved the ball through for a goal. The reaction from Selwood—who took a rare moment while lying on the ground to soak up the moment (he would later suggest it was the best goal he ever kicked)—and his family in the grandstand, who turned on the waterworks, sobbing uncontrollably, caused us to pause, blink, and wonder: do you think he's already decided?

Turns out, he had. He'd known for weeks. But, as was the Selwood way from the moment he arrived at Kardinia Park in late-2006, he wasn't interested in some song-and-dance-act farewell tour. Quite the opposite. While some close to Selwood, including an initially surprised and saddened coach Chris Scott, had known since before the round 23 clash with the Eagles that he would be hanging up his boots, most remained hopeful that, after another superb Grand Final performance, their revered leader would stick around in pursuit of the club's first back-to-back Premierships since 1951-52. Recalling what would be the last minutes of his career, Selwood, who was on the bench, seated between Sam De Koning and Mark Blicavs, before re-entering the fray, said: "Sam said, 'You can't finish'. My heart was racing, my eyes were watering. I knew I was going out for the last 15 minutes of my career." He paused and smiled, "I'm a bit soft".

As her husband embarked on a 15th finals campaign, even Brit Selwood would question whether they, as a couple—with a baby to come in February—had reached the right conclusion. Joel, too, had wondered whether he was making the right choice, but deep down he knew he couldn't guarantee the 100 per cent dedication he had given day after day, through glorious victories and heartbreaking defeats, for an unparalleled 355 games for the Cats (he had passed Corey Enright's 332 games in 2021's second semi-final), including a League-record 40 finals and a club-best four Premierships (2007, 2009, 2011 and 2022). Overlooked by a number of recruiters who felt the teenager's knees wouldn't withstand the wear and tear of a long career, Selwood not only survived—he excelled—and ultimately conquered the most uniquely demanding and taxing of sports. He became the face of a club (often bandaged and bloodied) that has evolved into one of the most admired sporting organisations in Australia. Chris Scott (pictured opposite with Selwood and chief executive Steve Hocking at the retirement announcement) put it simply: "He was the best representative of the Geelong footy club as you could imagine. He'll be irreplaceable. He's set up our footy club."

Aside from the Premierships, the six All-Australian jackets (2009-10, 2013-14, 2016-17), three 'Carji' Greeves Medals (2010, 2013-14), four AFLPA Robert Rose Most Courageous Player Awards (2009, 2012-14), a Ron Evans Medal as the NAB AFL Rising Star (2007) and numerous media awards, perhaps two accolades best summarise Selwood the player, the leader, the man. In 2022, Selwood passed Carlton champion Stephen Kernahan for most games as a VFL/AFL captain; his 245 games in charge will take some beating, as will his record of most wins as a captain (165). That he was thrice named All-Australian skipper (2013-14, 2016) says plenty about how others rated his leadership.

His special qualities of respect, honesty and sportsmanship, instilled in him by parents Maree and Bryce, and borne out of constant battles in the backyard with brothers Adam, Troy and Scott, were recognised in a different way this season when Selwood won the Jim Stynes Community Leadership Award for a commitment to serving those less advantaged. Being a role model comes naturally for Selwood. He embraces it and loves it. People gravitate towards him.

The Geelong Football Club has been Selwood's constant focus and support, as he said during his retirement announcement: "You don't come to the Geelong footy club to go to work for the money. You come for the experience, and I've loved every part of that." For the masses who enjoyed watching him work 'miracles' in body, mind and spirit since his debut in 2007, they will always be grateful for the way he guided them, finally, to footy's promised land.

When the inevitable retirement announcement came four days after the Grand Final, among the many who spoke in glowing terms of Selwood's legacy was Scott, "He's the best player I've ever seen." **G**

Dan Eddy

Ford

Ford
GFC
2007
Herald Sun

▲ **DUAL WINNER:** Throughout 2009, Geelong was hellbent on winning the Premiership they believed they'd lost through inaccurate kicking in the 2008 Grand Final loss to the Hawks. The Cats finished second on the ladder in '09, behind St Kilda, then defeated the Western Bulldogs (by 14 points) in the Qualifying Final before humiliating Collingwood (by 73 points) in the preliminary final. On a wet Grand Final day against the Saints, Joel Selwood had 25 disposals, five clearances and a goal to help his team overrun their opponents in a tense final quarter. The 12-point victory secured Selwood and Gary Ablett Jnr (pictured middle) a second Premiership after their 2007 success; for Cameron Mooney (right, holding son Jagger), who kicked five goals in the 2007 Premiership win, it meant a third Premiership medallion having previously played in North Melbourne's 1999 victory.

◀ **DREAM START:** Joel Selwood's debut season was certainly one to remember. He played 21 games in 2007, won the NAB AFL Rising Star award, and was a key member in Geelong's record-setting 119-point Grand Final victory over Port Adelaide. On that magical day, Selwood (pictured celebrating post-game with teammate Max Rooke) had 17 disposals, five clearances and seven inside-50s. The following year, when the heavily-fancied Cats were defeated by Hawthorn in the Grand Final, Selwood was one of his team's standouts, recording 29 disposals, six inside-50s and three tackles to earn two votes in the Norm Smith Medal.

TRIPLE TREAT: In a scene repeated in 2022, (pictured on pages eight and nine) Joel Selwood (with Tom Hawkins) got to parade the Premiership Cup in 2011. It was Selwood's third, after wins in 2007 and 2009, and Hawkins' second. Reigning Premier Collingwood entered the Grand Final as firm favourite and, by half-time, held a narrow lead. The Cats edged in front by three-quarter time, as Hawkins, Selwood and Jimmy Bartel all inspired their team, leading to a runaway 38-point victory. Hawkins monstered the Magpie defence to take nine marks and kick three goals, Bartel recorded 26 disposals and three goals, while Selwood had 28 disposals, seven tackles, six inside-50s and kicked two goals. When Norm Smith Medal votes were tallied, Bartel won the coveted award with 13 votes, ahead of Selwood (nine) and Hawkins (five).

Herald Sun
Herald Sun
Ford
GEELONG
CATS

FOOTY AND FAMILY: The best any parent can do is instil in their children good values, respect for all people, a strong work ethic and a never-die-wondering attitude. In that respect, Bryce (second from left) and Maree Selwood (third from right) have certainly played their roles. As was evident throughout their four sons' respective AFL careers, Scott (left), Joel (middle), and twins Troy (second right) and Adam (far right) all did their parents proud. Joel said at his farewell press conference, "My parents Bryce and Maree gave so much support in allowing me to chase my passions. Two of my brothers, Troy and Scott, spent time at the club

during my years here. That was a unique opportunity to blend footy and family. Adam has been a long way from home, having been in WA since 2002, but he has always been a huge supporter." Praising his wife Brit (pictured to Joel's right), Selwood said, "I owe Brit so much for the support and love she has given me. Brit, I love you and am excited for all the future holds for us." Brit posted on her social media afterwards, "You have made me, your family, friends, teammates and supporters so proud. You got your fairytale and it's just so fitting you leave the game this way. The biggest thing I'll miss is seeing you do something you love every day."

G

CROWNING GLORY

Geelong's dominant Premiership victory made it the seventh club to win at least 10 VFL/AFL Premierships. The victory also made it four wins in the national competition, matching the quartet won by the West Coast Eagles, but one in arrears of arch-rival Hawthorn's five.

Before becoming an inaugural member of the eight-club Victorian Football League at the end of 1896, Geelong was a powerhouse of the Victorian Football Association, winning seven Premierships before breaking away with seven other VFA clubs to form the new League.

Despite its lofty status and knack for success in the VFA, Geelong had to wait the best part of three decades (including missing the 1916 season during World War I because of a shortage of players) for its first League flag, which came in **1925** when the additions of Footscray, Hawthorn and North Melbourne saw the competition expand to 12 clubs (the inclusions of Richmond and University in 1908 had made it a 10-club competition until the end of 1914, when University withdrew). Playing in its maiden League Grand Final and led by captain-coach Cliff Rankin, Geelong was on top through to the last change before holding off a Collingwood comeback to win by 10 points.

After a loss to the great Collingwood 'Machine' team in the 1930 Grand Final, Geelong rebounded under the first-year coach Charlie Clymo in **1931** to beat Richmond by 20 points. It was the fourth meeting between the two clubs that season, with Geelong winning three including the decider.

In **1937** with the great Reg Hickey pulling the strings as captain-coach, Geelong would land flag number three after accounting for Collingwood by 32 points in front of a then-record crowd of 88,540 at the MCG in a contest lauded for the players' brilliant skills and speed. For decades the match was considered the Grand Final of all Grand Finals.

The **1951** win over Essendon, by 11 points, was the first leg of the club's only back-to-back triumph, which it completed in **1952** with an emphatic 46-point victory over the Magpies. After a break from the club, Hickey had returned in 1949 and immediately got the club back on track. Such was Geelong's dominance during this period—highlighted by a 26-match unbeaten streak that started early in the 1952 season and ended in round 14 the following year—it was in line to become just the fourth League club (after Carlton from 1906-08, Collingwood, 1927-30 and Melbourne,1939-41) to score a hat-trick of Premierships. But it wasn't to be, with inaccuracy in front of goal (8.17) contributing to the 12-point loss to Collingwood in the 1953 Grand Final.

Despite appearing in the next three finals series, Geelong would hit a rocky patch marked by consecutive wooden spoons and a slow five-year climb back up the ladder, culminating in **1963** with an impressive 49-point defeat of Hawthorn. It had been a close affair for the first three quarters, but the Cats were potent in the last term, brilliantly led to the club's sixth flag by the great Graham 'Polly' Farmer on the field and former great Bob Davis, 'the Geelong Flyer', as coach.

Geelong would remain supremely competitive for the next six seasons, finishing in the top four in each while winning 85 of 112 home-and-away matches. But the Cats lost a heartbreaker to Richmond in the 1967 Grand Final, sparking a streak of five straight losses in Grand Final appearances (1967, 1989, 1992, 1994-95), a run of outs that would end in **2007** with a record-setting 119-point demolition of Port Adelaide, the club's first Premiership in 44 years. The margin remains the greatest in a League Grand Final.

Under the coaching of Mark Thompson, the Cats were playing a high-possession, fast-and-furious style that countered the defence-first mode most other teams were employing at the time. Outfoxed and outplayed by the Hawks in the 2008 Grand Final, they rebounded in **2009** to win a nail-biter against St Kilda by 12 points, the outcome heavily shaped in a memorable moment that started in the middle of the ground late in the last quarter; with scores level, Matthew Scarlett and Gary Ablett cleverly combined to push the ball forward for Paul Chapman to goal. In the last tense six minutes, Geelong held the lead, eventually winning by 12 points.

In **2011**, with coach Chris Scott in his first season at the helm, the Cats made it three flags in a five-year span, defeating Collingwood against the odds. **G**

Peter Di Sisto

1925

SEPTEMBER 10, AT MCG

GEELONG	**3.2**	**7.8**	**10.13**	**10.19 (79)**
COLLINGWOOD	2.5	4.9	6.12	9.15 (69)

BACK ROW: Sid Hall, Jack Chambers, Denis Heagney, Lloyd Hagger, Bill Hudd, Arthur Coghlan, Stan Thomas.

SECOND ROW: Jack Paterson, George 'Jocka' Todd, Keith Johns, Eric Fleming, Tom Fitzmaurice, Dave Ferguson, Charlie Plane, Nick Brushfield, Jack Williams.

FRONT ROW: Frank Murrells, Edward Stevenson, Jockie Jones, Edward 'Carji' Greeves, Cliff Rankin (captain-coach), Les Smith, Arthur Rayson, Ken Leahy, Jim Warren.

BEST: Geelong – Chambers, Johns, Leahy, Rankin, Rayson, Warren. Collingwood – Chesswas, S. Coventry, Dibbs, Milburn, Stainsby, Webb.

GOALS: Geelong – Rankin 5, Chambers, Hagger, Hall, Heagney, Stevenson. Collingwood – F. Murphy 2, Stainsby 2, Webb 2, Baker, Chesswas, Tyson.

UMPIRE: J. McMurray snr.

ATTENDANCE: 64,288.

1931

SEPTEMBER 10, AT MCG

GEELONG	**2.3**	**5.6**	**8.11**	**9.14 (68)**
RICHMOND	1.2	4.5	5.5	7.6 (48)

BACK ROW: Ralph Lancaster, Joe Sellwood, Jack Williams, Bill Kuhlken, Jack Evans, Jack Walker, George Moloney, Edward 'Carji' Greeves.

THIRD ROW: Milton Lamb, Arthur Rayson, Jack Collins, Ted Llewellyn, Les Hardiman, Peter Hardiman, Bob Troughton.

SECOND ROW: Tommy Quinn, Rupe McDonald, George 'Jocka' Todd, Ted Baker (captain), Arthur Coghlan, Len Metherell, Reg Hickey, Frank Mockridge.

FRONT ROW: Jack Carney, Max Kelly.

BEST: Geelong – Hickey, Carney, Lamb, McDonald, P. Hardiman, Williams.
Richmond – O'Neill, Foster, Geddes, G. Strang, Zschech, Ford.

GOALS: Geelong – Metherell 2, Baker 2, L. Hardiman 2, Troughton, Collins, Moloney. Richmond – D. Strang 3, Titus 2, Ford, Twyford.

UMPIRE: R. Scott.

ATTENDANCE: 60,712.

1937

SEPTEMBER 25, AT MCG

GEELONG	**3.3**	**8.5**	**12.8**	**18.14 (122)**
COLLINGWOOD	6.3	8.10	11.14	12.18 (90)

BACK ROW: Bernie Miller, Jim Wills, Bill Dyer, Norm Glenister, Angie Muller, Leo Dean.

THIRD ROW: Stan Mullane, Allan Everett, Jack Evans, Clyde Helmer, Neil Tucker, Stan Howard, Laurie Slack.

SECOND ROW: Clive Coles, Jack Metherell, Geoff Mahon, Les Hardiman, Bernie Hore, Jack Grant, Fred Hawking, Ashley Foley.

FRONT ROW: Tom Arklay, Peter Hardiman, George Dougherty, Reg Hickey (captain-coach), Tommy Quinn, Gordon Abbott, Joe Sellwood.

BEST: Geelong – Muller, Quinn, L. Hardiman, P. Hardiman, J. Metherell. Collingwood – Regan, Froude, Ross, Todd, A. Collier, Woods.

GOALS: Geelong – Evans 6, J. Metherell 4, Coles 4, Abbott 2, Sellwood, Wills. Collingwood – Todd 4, G. Coventry 3, Pannam 2, Doherty, Kyne, Fothergill.

UMPIRE: G. Batt.

ATTENDANCE: 88,540.

1951

SEPTEMBER 29, AT MCG

GEELONG	**3.8**	**4.10**	**9.13**	**11.15 (81)**
ESSENDON	1.0	6.2	6.5	10.10 (70)

BACK ROW: Bruce Morrison, Alan Hickinbotham, Bob Davis, Loy Stewart, Russell Renfrey, George Goninon, Les Reed.

THIRD ROW: Russell Middlemiss, Bert Worner, Jim Norman, Bill McMaster, Tom Morrow, John Hyde, Norm Scott.

SECOND ROW: Terry Fulton, Leo Turner, Bernie Smith, Reg Hickey (coach), Fred Flanagan (captain), Syd Tate, Ron Hovey.

FRONT ROW: Neil Trezise, Peter Pianto.

BEST: Geelong - Morrison, B. Smith, McMaster, Turner, Hyde, Trezise. Essendon - Gardiner, Mann, N. McDonald, May, Syme, Bigelow.

GOALS: Geelong - Goninon 4, Davis, Pianto, McMaster, Turner, Flanagan, Morrow, Norman. Essendon - K. McDonald 2, Syme 2, May, Hutchison, Snell, Tate, Jones, Payne.

UMPIRE: H. Jamieson.

ATTENDANCE: 84,109.

1952

SEPTEMBER 27, AT MCG

GEELONG	**4.2**	**5.3**	**11.6**	**13.8 (86)**
COLLINGWOOD	1.1	3.3	5.4	5.10 (40)

BACK ROW: Leo Turner, Geoff Williams, John Hyde, Jim Norman, Russell Renfrey.

THIRD ROW: Bruce Morrison, Russell Middlemiss, Norm Sharp, Bill McMaster, George Goninon, Ron Hovey.

SECOND ROW: Peter Pianto, Neil Trezise, Fred Flanagan (captain), Bernie Smith, Terry Fulton, Sid Smith.

FRONT ROW: Doug Palmer, Bob Davis, Bert Worner.

BEST: Geelong - Williams, Trezise, Sharp, Goninon, B. Smith, Morrison. Collingwood - Merrett, Mann, R. Rose, Parker, Tuck, M. Twomey.

GOALS: Geelong - Goninon 5, Trezise 4, Davis, McMaster, Flanagan, Worner. Collingwood - Parker 3, Merrett 2.

UMPIRE: H. Jamieson.

ATTENDANCE: 81,304.

1963

OCTOBER 5, AT MCG

GEELONG	**3.3**	**7.10**	**9.13**	**15.19 (109)**
HAWTHORN	3.6	5.6	8.9	8.12 (60)

BACK ROW: Colin Rice, John Sharrock, John Watts, John Yeates, Geoff Rosenow, Roy West, Tony Polinelli.

SECOND ROW: Gordon Hynes, John Brown, Paul Vinar, Doug Wade, Ken Goodland, Peter Walker, Ian Scott, Hugh Routley.

FRONT ROW: Graham 'Polly' Farmer, Alistair Lord, John Devine, Bob Davis (coach). Fred Wooller (captain), Stewart Lord, Bill Goggin.

BEST: Geelong - Farmer, Devine, Scott, Goggin, Walker, Wooller. Hawthorn - Arthur, Nalder, Coverdale, Mort, Young, Youren.

GOALS: Geelong - Wooller 3, Hynes 3, Yeates 2, Goggin 2, Rice 2, A. Lord 2, Wade. Hawthorn - Peck 3, Woodley, Law, Coverdale, Mort, Fisher.

UMPIRE: J. Crouch.

ATTENDANCE: 101,452.

2007

SEPTEMBER 29, AT MCG

GEELONG	**5.7**	**11.13**	**18.17**	**24.19 (163)**
PORT ADELAIDE	2.2	4.3	5.5	6.8 (44)

BACK ROW: James Kelly, Josh Hunt, Matthew Scarlett, Nathan Ablett, Brad Ottens, Steven King, Steve Johnson, Andrew Mackie, Joel Corey, Cameron Mooney, Corey Enright, Jimmy Bartel, Darren Milburn.

FRONT ROW: David Wojcinski, Paul Chapman, Gary Ablett Jnr, Shannon Byrnes, Tom Harley (captain), Mark Thompson (coach), Cameron Ling, Max Rooke, Joel Selwood, Mathew Stokes.

BEST: Geelong - S. Johnson, Scarlett, Chapman, King, Enright, Mooney, Corey. Port Adelaide - C. Cornes, K. Cornes, P. Burgoyne.

GOALS: Geelong - Mooney 5, Chapman 4, S.Johnson 4, N. Ablett 3, Bartel 2, G. Ablett jnr, Mackie, Ottens, Rooke, Byrnes, Ling. Port Adelaide - S. Burgoyne 2, Tredrea 2, C. Cornes, Logan.

UMPIRES: S. McBurney, S. McInerney, S. McLaren.

ATTENDANCE: 97,302.

NORM SMITH MEDAL: Steve Johnson.

2009

SEPTEMBER 26, AT MCG

GEELONG	**3.0**	**7.1**	**9.4**	**12.8 (80)**
ST KILDA	3.2	7.7	9.11	9.14 (68)

BACK ROW: Joel Corey, Steve Johnson, James Kelly, Brad Ottens, Harry Taylor, Tom Hawkins, Andrew Mackie, Matthew Scarlett, Cameron Mooney, Mark Blake, Darren Milburn, Max Rooke, Corey Enright.

FRONT ROW: Travis Varcoe, Paul Chapman, Gary Ablett Jnr, Shannon Byrnes, Tom Harley (captain), Mark Thomson (coach), Cameron Ling, Joel Selwood, Jim Bartel, David Wojcinski.

BEST: Geelong - Chapman, Milburn, Ablett, Selwood, Bartel, Taylor, Corey. St Kilda - Gram, Hayes, Goddard, Baker, Montagna, Ball.

GOALS: Geelong - Chapman 3, Mooney 2, Hawkins 2, Rooke 2, Selwood, Byrnes, Ablett. St Kilda - Schneider 2, Hayes, Montagna, Riewoldt, Goddard, Kositchke, Dempster, Jones.

UMPIRES: S. McBurney, S. Ryan, B. Rosebury.

ATTENDANCE: 99,251

NORM SMITH MEDAL: Paul Chapman (Geelong).

2011

OCTOBER 1, AT MCG

GEELONG	**4.3**	**8.6**	**13.7**	**18.11 (119)**
COLLINGWOOD	4.2	9.3	12.6	12.9 (81)

BACK ROW: Steve Johnson, Joel Selwood, Joel Corey, Mitch Duncan, James Kelly, Harry Taylor, Andrew Mackie, Tom Hawkins, Tom Lonergan, Trent West, James Podsiadly, Matthew Scarlett, Brad Ottens, Joel Corey, Josh Hunt.

FRONT ROW: Travis Varcoe, Paul Chapman, David Wojcinski, Cameron Ling (captain), Chris Scott (coach), Jim Bartel, Allen Christensen, Mathew Stokes,

BEST: Geelong - Bartel, Selwood, Hawkins, Ling, S. Johnson, Lonergan, Chapman, Ottens, Varcoe, Mackie. Collingwood - Pendlebury, Thomas, Sidebottom, Tarrant, Ball, L. Brown, Johnson.

GOALS: Geelong - S. Johnson 4, Hawkins 3, Bartel 3, Varcoe 3, Selwood 2, Stokes, Duncan, Ling. Collingwood - Cloke 3, Krakouer 3, Sidebottom 2, Ball, Johnson, Wellingham, L. Brown.

SUBSTITUTES: Duncan (Geelong), Fasolo (Coll).

UMPIRES: C. Donlon, S. Ryan, B. Rosebury.

ATTENDANCE: 99,537.

NORM SMITH MEDAL: Jim Bartel (Geelong).

GRAND FINAL

September 24, 2022

Attendance: 100,024

At the Melbourne Cricket Ground

GEELONG 20.13 (133) D SYDNEY SWANS 8.4 (52)

QUARTER BY QUARTER

GEELONG	6.5	9.8	15.11	20.13 (133)
SYDNEY	1.0	4.2	4.3	8.4 (52)

BEST

GEELONG: Smith, Dangerfield, Stengle, Hawkins, Selwood, Close, Blicavs, Duncan.

GOALS

GEELONG: Stengle 4, Hawkins 3, Smith 3, Cameron 2, Close 2, Blicavs, De Koning, Duncan, C. Guthrie, Parfitt, Selwood.

THE LINE-UPS (AS NAMED):

GEEL	**FB**	Sam De Koning (16)	Jack Henry (38)	Jake Kolodjashnij (8)
SYD	**FF**	Ryan Clarke (4)	Lance Franklin (23)	Will Hayward (9)
GEEL	**HB**	Tom Stewart (44)	Zach Tuohy (2)	Jed Bews (24)
SYD	**HF**	Isaac Heeney (5)	Sam Reid (20)	Tom Papley (11)
GEEL	**C**	Mark Blicavs (46)	Mark O'Connor (42)	Mitch Duncan (22)
SYD	**C**	Justin McInerney (27)	Luke Parker (26)	Dylan Stephens (3)
GEEL	**HF**	Brad Close (45)	Jeremy Cameron (5)	Isaac Smith (7)
SYD	**HB**	Nick Blakey (22)	Robbie Fox (42)	Oliver Florent (13)
GEEL	**FF**	Tyson Stengle (18)	Tom Hawkins (26)	Gary Rohan (23)
SYD	**FB**	Jake Lloyd (44)	Dane Rampe (24)	Tom McCartin (30)
GEEL	**FOL**	Rhys Stanley (1)	Patrick Dangerfield (35)	Cameron Guthrie (29)
SYD	**FOL**	Tom Hickey (31)	James Rowbottom (8)	Callum Mills (14)
GEEL	**IC**	Joel Selwood (14) Gryan Miers (32)	Tom Atkins (30) Zach Guthrie (39)	**MEDICAL SUB** Brandan Parfitt (3)
SYD	**IC**	Chad Warner (1) Errol Gulden (21)	Hayden McLean (2) Paddy McCartin (39)	**MEDICAL SUB** Braedan Campbell (16)
GEEL	**COACH**	Chris Scott		
SYD	**COACH**	John Longmire		

EMERGENCIES:
GEEL: Sam Menegola (27), Jonathon Ceglar (15)
SYD: Harry Cunningham (7), Logan McDonald (6), Will Gould (17)
UMPIRES: Jacob Mollison, Brett Rosebury, Matt Stevic

Note: Max Holmes was originally named on the interchange bench but was a late withdrawal because of injury incurred in the preliminary final. Mark O'Connor (originally listed as the medical sub) was elevated to the starting team while Brandan Parfitt (originally picked as an emergency) was named the medical sub after Holmes' withdrawal. The reshuffling left Geelong with two emergencies, Sam Menegola and Jonathon Ceglar. Ceglar had also been an emergency for Hawthorn when Hawthorn won the 2014 and 2015 Premierships.

DADDY!: Mitch Duncan greets his children Scarlett and Archie on the MCG as the post-Premiership celebrations gain momentum.

22
Ford

BY THE NUMBERS

1 Norm Smith medallist—Isaac Smith, who polled 14 of the maximum 15 votes from the five judges. Teammate Patrick Dangerfield received 10, the second-most.

2 Jock McHale medals—Despite winning a Premiership in his first season as coach (2011) and having an impressive winning percentage of 71.3 (204 wins from 286 matches), coach Chris Scott has attracted his share of criticism in his 12-season tenure at the Cats. A second Jock McHale Medal as Premiership coach has silenced the doubters.

3 Tom Hawkins (67 goals), Jeremy Cameron (65) and Tyson Stengle (53) booted 50-plus goals in 2022, the first time three Cats have achieved this in the same season.

4 The number of players who wore a jumper number higher than 40 on Grand Final day, the most in a Premiership team. Mark O'Connor (42), Tom Stewart (44), Brad Close (45) and Mark Blicavs (46) combined to set the new mark.

5 Cats were selected in the 2022 All-Australian team: Tom Stewart, Jeremy Cameron, Tom Hawkins (captain), Tyson Stengle and Mark Blicavs. For the second year in a row, the All-Australian captain played in the Premiership team, with Melbourne's Max Gawn achieving the honour in 2021.

6 The number of Grand Finals Geelong's skipper Joel Selwood has played in. The Cats' games record holder (355) has played in Geelong's 2007, 2009, 2011 and 2022 Premierships, as well as the losing Grand Finals of 2008 and 2020. He now has the record number of finals appearances (40), passing Hawthorn champion Michael Tuck's mark, set in 1991.

7 The number of scoring assists Patrick Dangerfield recorded in the Grand Final, resulting in six goals and a behind. His effort was the best in an AFL final since 2003, when the statistic was first officially recorded.

8 The number of times the Cats finished a round on top of the ladder in 2022. Geelong headed the field after round one but did not top the table again until round 17. The Cats would not relinquish top spot after that.

9 Max Holmes established himself as a permanent part of Geelong's back six in the second half of 2022, but a strained hamstring meant the Cats' No. 9 had to watch from the sidelines as his teammates stormed to a Premiership.

10 Geelong has now won 10 VFL/AFL Premierships, joining Carlton and Essendon (16 apiece), Collingwood (15), and Hawthorn, Richmond and Melbourne (13 apiece) in double figures. Geelong had also won seven Premierships in the pre-VFL period (1870 to 1896).

10 The number of players aged over 30 in Geelong's flag-winning side. The Sydney Swans had four in the Grand Final.

11 The number of years between Premierships for coach Chris Scott, then in his first season, and players Joel Selwood, Tom Hawkins and Mitch Duncan.

16 The Grand Final triumph was the Cats' 16th consecutive win. Their last loss in 2022 came against St Kilda, on May 14, in round nine.

19 Tom Hawkins ended the season with 67 goals and in 19th place on the all-time VFL/AFL goalkickers list, with 732. Both Hawkins and Jeremy Cameron (65) led the season's goalkicking table, but Carlton's Charlie Curnow was the Coleman medallist with 64 in the home and away season.

25 The number of games Geelong played in 2022, with Tom Atkins, Brad Close, Cam Guthrie, Tom Hawkins and Tyson Stengle featuring in all 25.

28 plus **206** The average age in years and days of the Cats' Grand Final-winning team, the oldest in any VFL/AFL match played. The average games played was 167.6, marginally ahead of Hawthorn's 2015 team (166.8). In 2011, Geelong's Premier team's average age was 27 years, 99 days, and average games played 146.

35 Players pulled on the boots at least once for the Cats in 2022, with four making their debut.

41 Geelong's score of 6.5 (41) at the first break was the highest quarter-time score, and margin (35 points), in a Grand Final since 1989, when Hawthorn registered 8.4 (52), and led by 40 points, coincidentally against the Cats.

70 The number of years since Geelong has won a Premiership in an even year. The Cats' fifth flag win came in 1952. All of their other Grand Final wins came in odd years—1925, 1931, 1937, 1951, 1963, 2007, 2009 and 2011.

81 The Cats' winning margin was the fifth highest in League Grand Final history. Geelong holds the gold medal with their 119-point victory over Port Adelaide in 2007.

111 Geelong's biggest loss of 2022 was by 30 points, ironically against their Grand Final opponents Sydney in round two at the SCG. The Grand Final margin of 81 points represents a turnaround of 111 points between their two meetings this season.

144.22 The Cats' percentage at the end of the home-and-away season was the season's highest by a clear margin, ahead of Melbourne's 130.55. Geelong, with 2146 points, ranked third in the AFL for 'points for' (behind Richmond, 2165 and Brisbane, 2146), and third for 'points conceded' 1488, (behind Melbourne, 1483 and Fremantle, 1486).

184 Marks taken through the season by veteran Mitch Duncan, the most of any Cat in 2022, ahead of Isaac Smith (161) and Tom Stewart (146).

157 Tackles laid by Tom Atkins in season 2022. Previously used mainly as a lockdown defender, Atkins blossomed with a move to the midfield this year.

1092 The number of days between the 2022 Grand Final and the previous one played at the MCG. COVID-19 kept footy's biggest day away from Melbourne in 2020 (held at the Gabba in Brisbane) and 2021 (Optus Oval, Perth).

Hardie Grant

BOOKS

Produced in 2022 by the Slattery Media Group for Hardie Grant Books

Published in 2022 by Hardie Grant Books, an imprint of Hardie Grant Publishing

Hardie Grant Books (Melbourne)
Wurundjeri Country
Building 1, 658 Church Street
Richmond, Victoria 3121

Hardie Grant Books (London)
5th & 6th Floors
52–54 Southwark Street
London SE1 1UN

hardiegrant.com/books

Hardie Grant acknowledges the Traditional Owners of the Country on which we work, the Wurundjeri People of the Kulin Nation and the Gadigal People of the Eora nation, and recognises their continuing connection to the land, waters and culture. We pay our respects to their Elders past and present.

Australian Football League
AFL House, 140 Harbour Esplanade, Docklands, Victoria, Australia, 3008.

A catalogue record for this book is available from the National Library of Australia

We Are Geelong The pictorial story of Geelong's campaign to win a 10th VFL/AFL Premiership

SOFT COVER
ISBN 9781 74379 9529
10 9 8 7 6 5 4 3 2 1

The publisher wishes to thank the Geelong Football Club for its support with this publication.

Prints of photographs published in **We Are Geelong** can be purchased at aflphotos.com.au.

Publisher: Pam Brewster
Editor: Geoff Slattery
Managing Editor: Penelope White
Design Manager: Kristin Thomas
Designer: Craig Poore for the Slattery Media Group
Writers: Peter Di Sisto, Dan Eddy, Andrew Gigacz, Geoff Slattery
Photo Editor: Natalie Boccassini
Production Manager: Todd Rechner
Production Coordinator: Jessica Harvie

Printed by Finsbury Green Pty Ltd